WHAT'S YOUR NAME I'M FINE THANK YOU

WHAT'S YOUR NAME I'M FINE THANK YOU

MUGGED BY REALITY IN BANGKOK AND BEYOND

Roger Beaumont

ASIA BOOKS

These articles were originally published in *Bangkok Metro* magazine and *The Nation* newspaper, and some have been re-edited for this collection.

Published and Distributed by
Asia Books Co. Ltd.,
5 Sukhumvit Road Soi 61,
PO Box 40,
Bangkok 10110,
Thailand.
Tel: (66) 0-2714-0740 ext. 3202–4
Fax: (66) 0-2714-2799
E-mail: information@asiabooks-thailand.com
Website: asiabooks-thailand.com

Fourth printing, 2002

All Illustrations by Hann Win

Typeset by COMSET
Printed by Darnsutha Press Co., Ltd.

ISBN 974-8237-11-7

For
Yueh Ching Chen

Contents

Introduction ix
Acknowledgements xi

Deep in the Heart of Bangkok, Texas 1
Love Thy Neighbour 6
Nomads, Zen and Now 9
A Suitable State of Mind 12
And the First Shall Be the Last 15
I Gave You the Best Ears of My Life 19
Elvis Spotted in Hilltribes 24
Still Waiting Sir 27
Oscar Bait 32
Things Are Looking Up 35
Flood and Be Damned 38
The Horse Yeller 41
You've Either Got it or You Ain't 46
Lead Us Not into Temptation 50
Love and Illusion 53
Across the Baize 56

Contents

All Aboard the Feral Express 61

Australia: Top Breeders Recommend it 64

Veni, Vidi, Versace 68

Stiff Upper Brits 72

New Age Gunpowder Plot 76

Psst! Bubonic Plague! Pass it On! 79

Christmas Past 82

The Business of Pleasure 85

A Class Apart 90

Thongs for the Memory 98

Are You Sitting Comfortably? 101

Desperate Dispatches 105

Desperately Seeking Sustenance 108

Diary of a Sane Man 111

New Year Anyone? 115

Jungle Fever 118

Made in England 122

Opium, Visas, and the Dead 126

More 'E' Vicar 131

When Kush Comes to Shove 136

Any Which Way but Up 141

Unplugged and Unstamped 145

Resting between Challenges 149

"Air Raid Live Tonight! Admission
    Free for Prisoners" 152

Soup, Debt, and Effort 156

Position Wanted: Anywhere but Here 159

A Cheque in the Right Direction 166

The Xmas Files 1997 172

Wealth Behaving Badly 177

Caught in the Fact 182

Introduction

It's not always easy to seek for the truth in humour and for the humour in truth. Ask Roger Beaumont, who defies the adage that if you remember the sixties, you weren't there. His memories of people, cities, and travel are vivid. Some of them may even resemble the way events actually happened.

What follows, in episodes that won't take any longer to read than it takes to down a cold beer, is a sort of auto-biography, in which Mr. Beaumont left his native England in search of a guru in India, and found the Wizard of Ooze in Bangkok instead. There are 46 stories in all, originally published in *Bangkok Metro* magazine, and *The Nation* newspaper.

Every one, seamless even when chaotic and off-the-wall, is a carefully polished gem, reminiscent of essays by America's S. J. Perelman and Robert Benchley—humorists even he's too young to remember. Influences, he says, are the American novelist Tom Robbins, along with British writers Laurence Norfolk, Bruce Chatwin, and Julian Barnes.

Introduction

Roger confessed that he was once a hippie, but a realistic one, which, I suppose, is why his monthly features in *Metro* for two years were called "Mugged by Reality." That his features in *The Nation* appear under the title "Slightly Out of Focus" provides another clue.

"I'm a foreigner dealing with the paradoxes and realities of living here," he says. "My intention is to try to explain how absurd and magical this place is—what it does to me and what it does to others. It holds me, this city."

Certainly, he's had other choices. Brought up in, and expelled from, a public school [read, fee-paying, private school] in Yorkshire, he found himself next in an international school in Rome, sitting next to Dylan Thomas's son. For several years he wandered, mainly in Asia, eventually spending nine years as a professional musician in Australia before coming to Thailand six years ago.

There is a connection between his music and his writing. "You've got to get it in the first paragraph," he says. "You have to demand the reader's attention. It's like what Sting said about rock and roll: 'It has to burn from the very first chord.'"

Roger does that. He is, in a way, a child of Dickens, whose message was, "Economy, economy." Make every word count, for brevity is the sister of talent. Roger takes his writing seriously.

The best part, for us, is that he never takes himself seriously.

Jerry Hopkins
Author of *No one Gets Out of Here Alive*
Bangkok, 1998.

Acknowledgements

I'd like to thank:

David Judge for helping me to see that information technology might be a royal road to the truth; Bob Garlick, creative director, who believes all things are possible *and* stress-free; Rich Baker for his patient skill in corralling my ramblings; Luci Standley for her sweet loyalty and desperate loans; Dave Johnson for his support and brotherhood; John Twigg and Philip Cornwel-Smith for giving me a break at *Bangkok Metro*; Nithinand Yorsaengrat for having faith in me at *The Nation*; Hann Win for his human insight and marvelous art; Jerry Hopkins for his sharp discourse and guidance; Josh for his jazz; Lim for hanging in and growing up; Claire Barron for always sending in my copy two nano-seconds before deadline so that no one else could fiddle with it; and finally, my Mum, for leaving all those *National Geographics* lying ar ound.

Roger Beaumont,
December, 1998.

Deep in the Heart
of Bangkok, Texas

To most expats in Bangkok, Washington Square was a cinema where movies could be seen in English, the billboard was usually spelt wrong, and dogs of questionable character and motive slept on the steps. I know, because one bit me. The anti-rabies injections cost 3,000 baht.

The dog's still alive—and worth about a dollar—and lies waiting for me in a fake siesta by the abandoned popcorn stand. Warning!

But there's another, extraordinary world here hidden among the cracked and faded concrete along the eastern side of the cinema. Spread over three nondescript bars called The Silver Dollar, Texas Lonestar, and The Wild Country, is an enclave of America that I always thought existed, but only in other people's imagination.

On the surface, this compact environment is a world of country 'n' western, loud voices, bad vowels, the good, the bad, and the facially challenged. It's frequented by an endless stream of oil workers on R 'n' R, retirees who saw service in Korea and Vietnam, and those who didn't see anything anywhere except Patpong in a drunken haze at the height of the war, and then stayed on for the next twenty years.

There's endless banter recalling "home," as well as complaints about Bangkok and the alleged deviousness of the people they live amongst—or rather don't. Local reality seems to have escaped their notice, and Thailand is another country somewhere else. They have no interest in the culture other than a lifestyle that offers available women, a little business, and cheap rent in a decadent exile. While many have married Thai women, you never see them. Bars aren't for women; well, certainly not your own, and certainly not here.

It's a place where gossip is ripe, yet the truth a fluid concept—and intelligence appears to hum along at a redneck pace slightly below room temperature. It's a bonfire of profanities. It brims with large, bellicose men who "know the price of everything and the value of nothing," as Oscar Wilde once said.

To these men, Vivaldi was not a musician, he's a gay bartender in Patpong. This environment doesn't attract attention to itself, doesn't advertise, neither needs nor wants the tourist trade, is self-contained, self-righteous, fascinating, and a fire escape to nowhere. And it became my home.

I lived above the Texas Lonestar for over a year. I am English, and to compound this problem I'm also a guitar player with my own hair. When I checked in, I felt about as popular as a vegetarian at a Dallas barbecue.

"Hey hippy, whyya grow ya hair so goddam long?" asked a bald, ageing vet' with a smirk.

"Because I can," I replied with an innocent expression.

Washington Square is a place of legends, both real and imaginary; the men who tell the stories that become the legends, and the legends that become the men who tell them: Yarns from deserts in Saudi, from freezing oil rigs in Northern Russia, of battles half remembered, and of women long departed but still vivid in the memory (and if slightly embellished, what the hell); stories of very serious money earned, won, and lost; men with larger-than-life characters who know their own destinies but argue with them just the same; tales of Laos during the war; the Death Railway; the CIA; the Contra arms deal; Beirut; the Gulf War; Red Adair; and of advice to presidents, monarchs, and dictators.

When the night manager of the Lonestar discovered I liked Miles Davis, I thought he was going to shoot me. Instead, I found an important ally. He put a black arm around my shoulder and said, "Mah *maan*!"

I was in. Into what, I had no idea, but I was in. When I tentatively enquired as to the validity of these stories, he shrugged and said, "*Shoot* boy! These guys are for real. The man sitting next to you was once the personal press secretary to Reagan. Ask him."

I did. He was. Well, that's what he said.

The average age is early fifties, and amidst the raucous anecdotes and serious drinking—"you gotta *learn* how to drink here, boy!"—there are men of quiet authority and Southern manners; serious achievers with thousand-yard stares and lived-in faces that speak of hard, disciplined lives, and upright integrity. They are well-earthed, experienced, hard to impress. They have a regular pulse. There is blood in their alcohol. They don't look for company but will accept it as long as you don't talk bullshit or golf. Their heroes are country 'n' western singers, football players, former presidents, dead generals, men who work the land, and men who truck the produce.

A sign in the Lonestar reads, "*For those who fought for it, freedom has a taste the protected will never know.*" These are proud men, and although America is resented as a place of abode—its society "shot through with drugs, violence, an' welfare"—the country's character is rigorously defended. Its influence on the world rests easy in their souls; its spirit and culture as sacred as a Harley-sized Smith and Wesson.

3

To such men, these bars represent a taste of home, a sense of bonding and of comfort. You can smell the T-bone, feel the bourbon, fool with the women.

"You leave tip for me pleez?"

"Sure honey. Buy low, sell high."

It's a man's world. Michael Jackson is a "faggot," Clinton a young "dumbass." The only thing they have in common with the president is a taste for cigars—and where to put them. Naturally, they have never inhaled.

These men aren't in Bangkok for any altruistic reasons. There are no budding monks, no spiritual journeys. Some came to make money, some to spend it, many to waste it on a lifestyle they couldn't get away with anywhere else. I've seen money change hands over a single NBA game that an English teacher could only dream of making even if he taught Big Bird to Korean rich-kids for the next millennium.

And then there are those poor souls who've been deprived of alcohol and female company by the sheer geography of their work, and arrive in town on a mission—which usually means a serious demonstration against sobriety.

I've seen the door at the Lonestar nearly ripped off its hinges as some madman—usually six foot four, wild-eyed, and crazed after six months in some scorching desert fixing giant earthmovers—hits the bar with a thirst that would make a camel blush.

One such character—let's call him "Crazy John"—who looks remarkably like a creature left over from the eighth episode of *Star Trek*, drank with intent for 72 hours on arrival.

The night manager and I found him in an alcoholic stupor halfway up the stairs at three in the morning in a position only a yoga master could appreciate—stark naked and legs akimbo.

"Mah man, we gotta get a doctor!"

"No," I said. "We gotta get a *camera*!"

4

And we did.

As in any community, the eccentrics and casualties balance out the seemingly stable and the relatively sober. These bars aren't only a unique microcosm of America, they're also another rich vein of expat life in this city. It may a potting shed to some, but you can find lots of things in potting sheds. I came across it by mistake, and left a year later blinking in the harsh sunlight of reality. I went back to Thailand—which was just outside the door. I made many friends, many contacts, worked hard, ate sensibly, and drank like a fish—deep in the heart of Bangkok, Texas.

We come to new countries intending to do certain things, and then a whole lot of different things happen. I like that.

Only once in the entire year did I come close to death. It was late. The bar was packed, primed, and loud. It was someone's birthday. Everyone was very drunk and I kept bumping into old acquaintances who didn't recognise me, and total strangers who did. Some cowboy was wailing through the sound system and I said far too loudly that country 'n' western was just, "Three chords and a cloud of dust."

There was a deathly silence. I froze in terror. I had realised my mistake. But it was too late. I had trodden on sacred ground. I had insulted their holy music. It was like passing wind very loudly in the Vatican and then giggling.

Suddenly the bar was humming with outrage. Someone yelled, "Shoot the sonofabitch!"—which soon turned into a chorus. Visualising a rope being thrown over a branch, I did the only thing left open to me. I rang the bar bell.

The drinks bill was so high it should have been delivered by a priest. I was still paying it off a year later. But hey, I'm alive. And grateful. And if you don't believe any of this, then I've got a bridge to sell you in Brooklyn.

Now all I have to do is to keep my eye on that damned dog.

Love Thy Neighbour

"Yes we have apartmen'. You fine it top stair. Loom ereven," she said.

To me, the image of an "apartmen'" has always conveyed comfort, income, decency.

But as I headed along the dark corridors and up the dilapidated stairs, it reminded me of a tenement block in a Gothic horror movie. It was full of alien noises. Screams uttered in strange languages from behind shut doors competed with glasses smashed in anger and purpose. There were thumps, moans, and bad stereos.

Through an open door I saw a video playing. There was no dialogue, just the exchange of gunfire. Cockroaches scattered in all directions at my approach. I stepped over a naked man who was asleep on the fourth floor. It was as if the devil himself was unchained and roaming about—and this was just the *public* area. Strangely, I felt right at home.

I opened the door numbered "ereven" only to find two prostitutes and a small frog watching television. None of them looked up when I entered. Then the frog slowly turned his little head towards me, clearly annoyed, and with a bulbous expression that seemed to say, "Hey man! Can't you *see* we are watching the programme?" hopped a foot to the right and then turned back to the screen.

I kicked the girls out and moved in with the frog. I called him Simpson. He ate insect wings and gooey alien things, and a week later I ate his legs, washed down with some *Chardonnay*. Finally, I had the place to myself.

Within a week I had met everyone in the block. I heard the tenant above me many times before I saw him. His door was always open and he was never alone.

"I shall never forget," I heard him say to an invisible guest, "how young Jack single-handedly stopped in its tracks, a particularly ugly-looking raiding party of *Mbobo* warriors; how he emerged from our hut unarmed, alone, and in cricket whites, and how their war-whoops fell silent as they dropped their weapons and slowly approached, fascinated . . ."

His name was Russell, he was sixty and holding, but he'd completely lost the plot. I liked him. But, like the frog, he was on his last legs here. He had lost his only means of income when his one Thai student of English confronted him with a newspaper, furiously stabbed at the sports headline "PIGGOT PRONOUNCED WINNER!" then yelled, "This bullshit language! You no good teacher!" and fled.

Russell had a talent for society, but no talent for poverty. He had a wealth of experience, but no experience of wealth, and like so many in the block, he was frustrated by the past and had difficulty with the now. He wore glasses that an ambitious optician had recommended, and he was dismayed when everyone nicknamed him the "Aviator." He had a growth above his top lip that could have been a moustache, but actually resembled an escaped ferret hiding under his nose. His ambition was to die magnificently in debt, and he slipped away one night without paying the rent.

And then there was Celine. She lived next door. A woman of paralysing beauty, she had a Balinese mother, a French father, and, unfortunately, a Swiss boyfriend. I adored her. She was held together by class rather than position, whereas I am held together by habit rather than health.

One day she said, "There's a tiny lizard living in my shower."

"Does it bother you?" I asked.

"No, I just wonder what it's living on."

"Love?" I suggested.

Her boyfriend is charming, rich, and rarely here. I dream evilly of skiing accidents.

There was an Australian girl who lived in room number seven who's hair was gelled and teased beyond repair. She was trying to start a magazine called *Creative Menopause*, and had posters on her wall advertising dismal events that dripped blood and CNN. She called herself a "liberal revolutionary."

"What's *that*?" I asked.

"It means I'll burn down your city and then offer to help with the rebuilding costs."

And so to Renzo, who came here to die. Bruised beyond repair by the Vietnam War, he came to Bangkok to see himself out. He called me Feliciano and was always asking, "Where's de goddam *maid*?"

Early one morning, a sheet was placed over him to keep him warm, and that sheet became his shroud. His last words on this planet were, "I'll see you downstairs in the bar."

But he never made it. I miss him, and so do many others.

Peter Ustinov once said that our friends are not necessarily the people we like the most, they're just the ones who got there first.

But neighbours?

That will always remain a raffle of humanity; a constant surprise—and they're living right next to you right now.

Nomads, Zen and Now

It's all Uncle Mac's fault. And it started on the 1st of February 1951. "Well, that's it. I'm off," he said to my father in a casual, laid-back way that suggested he was just popping out for a pint of milk.

He then climbed into his Land Rover, checked that he had his sandwiches and a thermos of tea, and set off for India. He reached Herat, Afghanistan, where he traded the vehicle for a horse, and headed east. And he was never heard of again.

A rumoured sighting of him on the Great Wall of China in the early seventies by an old RAF chum gave a ray of hope—but then again, he thought he saw him accompanied by Richard Nixon, Shirley Maclaine, and Keith Richards. Well, it's *that* kind of wall.

My father lost a brother, and I lost a hero and I wasn't even born yet. His journey continued to fascinate me as I grew up. Just getting to India alone, exposed, and overland in 1951 would have been an achievement. No video bars or guesthouses. His reasons for going were even more intriguing. There weren't any. He just went. Now *that* is travel.

9

I was born within shouting distance of Hadrian's Wall—that last bit of serious landscaping on the edge of the Roman Empire. What the Roman scouts thought when they saw their first Scot was similar to going to a Black Sabbath concert. They threw up and ran like hell. Hairy, tough, covered in woad, carrying serious weapons, wearing skirts, and muttering, "I'll 'av *yoo* Jimmy," was quite enough.

"Seal the borders," was the order from Rome. And they did. To us, Scotland was cold, misty, and, well, weird. To them, England was frippery, poncey lords, and warm beer. But it didn't stop them from slipping over the wall, nicking all our women, and smoking all our dope. If you argued, you got a face full of axe and a head-butt. Whether the wall was to keep them out or to keep them in is debatable—and irrelevant. They escaped anyway.

Scots are to be found from Archangel to Antarctica, and do you know why the British Empire got so big? It was a nation desperately looking for a decent meal. By the way, have you tried haggis?

Don't.

My uncle escaped, and twenty years later, I picked myself up off a Greek island and followed his trail. A rickety ship from Istanbul to Trabzon; public bus from Erzerum to Iraq; and train, bus, and camel across Iran. The first white person I spoke to after four months was in Isfahan. He was a Scot, who said over a plate of sheep's eyeballs, "We used to *eat* Englishmen."

I got shot on a bus in Herat, I got lost in Pakistan, and when I finally made it to Macleod Gunj (which is not a Scottish garage band from Seattle) in Northern India, I asked to see the Dalai Lama.

"He's in Dublin," I was informed by a beaming monk.

Damn. I thought I deserved instant enlightenment for just *reaching* the place.

Doesn't anyone stay in one place anymore? The answer then and now, is no. Where the hell is everyone? Escaping. Nomading.

The two young lads I met on the train from Penang to Bangkok last week are the new nomads. One of them was wearing baggy shorts and purple wrap-around Raybans, and was eating some disgusting local insects out of a bag.

"*Greeet* mon!" he said, crunching away. His mate had spiky, multi-coloured hair which looked as though a bird of paradise had landed on his head and someone had smashed it with a mallet. They were from Glasgow.

Their tale was of comparing Hard Rock Cafes and Pizza Huts, and bungy jumps and video bars in the different countries they'd travelled to. They longed to visit places where they weren't expected, and mourned the fact that the whole planet appeared to be one vast, soulless shopping mall. They thought I was a "lucky bastard" for having been able to visit places before American culture did.

I resent being called lucky.

They assumed their children would vacation in the land of virtual reality rather than cross the Gobi desert single-handed, or wrestle with pygmies and win.

But opportunities still exist. After all, it's now possible to drive from The Great Wall to Hadrian's Wall without getting out of the car. You could be greeted with, "We used to de-bone Chinamen, Jimmy!" THWACK!

I mean, who'd want to miss that?

A Suitable
State of Mind

I was always taught that good judgement comes fr om experience, and that experience comes from bad judgement. I therefore claim August in Bangkok as "Survivors Month." It rains. Potential visitors are elsewhere chasing sun.

Let's be real. Bangkok is a Thai city with a few foreigners thrown in for flavour. Occasionally a few are thrown out when they're out of favour, yet anyone who has ever read this column will know that its sentiments identify most with those who came here of their own volition, put whatever it was they had on the table, and either sunk or swum, lied or strived, or—as is more often the case—all of the above.

As the country is moving faster than history, those who venture here find out very quickly who they are. And even faster, who they are not.

This city has an addictive quality that leaves few certainties intact. If you have a character, it will be enhanced; if you don't, then the airport's just up the road. This group of oddballs may a be ragtag league that doesn't fit comfortably with expat sensibilities—but maybe that's why I like it so much. It's so weird, it's practically an elite. It's refreshingly resilient and individual, and the bullshit is at least familiar—and often amusing.

The generation who came here before the current crop of misfits certainly had to pay their dues, but I would say—despite their wisdom and bluster—that they had it much easier. For the survivor today, pessimism is a luxury that is unaffordable. One has to stay sharp. I know I'm losing my edge when people ask to borrow money—because they've beaten me to the question.

How to deal with the reality of living here? Shall we call in the experts, or shall we just screw it up ourselves?

For some people, every problem is a calamity; it's not a challenge, it's a crisis with a party hat. Their needs never change—they are either urgent or desperate. Some even revert to counseling—but then I have always held that counseling is to personal problems what the Belgian army was to Hitler.

Others live at ease with the obscurity for which nature has designed them. There are many who cannot stand the heat, pollution, and corruption. To them I would say, I refuse to treat my health as a disease—and corruption is fun if you're placed right. A friend perceptively remarked, "I can't imagine living in Bangkok. But then I can't imagine living anywhere else either."

Sometimes we are besieged by an opposing elite—from another direction, and of a different character. It's the annual visit from those who come from London, LA, Munich, or Manchester. They bulge with obscene amounts of money, leave responsibility somewhere over the Himalayas, land in Thailand, and then party with a vengeance. Their first day in Bangkok is a bit like the last day on the *Titanic*. Mayhem.

I was so broke when I arrived, I could hardly afford to walk home—and I used to be envious of them. But then I'm used to poverty, as I come from a country that's been broke for years.

Yet as things turned around for me, I found the habits of the perennial visitors did not. Their first week is usually chaos, and their last week is the first week in reverse. Their bonhomie can often be superficial, and they tend to bring out the best in others, only to bring out the worst in themselves. They go to a bar, make two new friends, and lose five old ones. Leaning over vodka-soaked counters, some even talk about the chemistry between people—when what they really mean is, a similar taste in narcotics.

Then they tell us survivors how we should live and how little we are making—while they themselves leave a trail of mess, debts, and broken hearts, and go home.

There is a Japanese proverb:

First the man takes a drink,

Then the drink takes a drink,

And then the drink takes the man.

Resident survival skills are also far from perfect. I always thought I was surrounded by annoying characters called Simon "Can-you-lend-me-500-till-Friday" Webster—until I discovered I was one of them. The pretence of an honest upward mobility came home when somebody approached me in a bar and said, "Is your name Roger?" and I replied, "No, I'm just breaking it in for a friend."

So, if you wake up one morning and find yourself fishing for condoms in a *klong*, and you really have lost the plot, don't worry—there'll be another one along in a minute.

A friend telephoned from Bali last week and said, "What shall I bring?"

And I answered without hesitation:

"Money and a suitable state of mind."

And the First
Shall Be the Last

Ask any traveller what they remember about a country and invariably it's their first impressions that remain the most vivid. Undoubtedly, this is due to a heightening of the senses. The smells, tastes, colours, and language are all registered with a freshness, simply because they *are* foreign.

Depending on the degree of cultural shock, the traveller's mouth can spend more time open than shut. Not in speech, but amazement.

But, over time, the excitement wanes, those mental photo negatives become faded, and the owner of them often becomes jaded. A natural consequence of experience.

Arriving at midnight in this country, my first impression was not simply of the number of cars on the road—but at how badly they were being driven. Heading into the city, my taxi passed another one in flames, lying mortally wounded by the side of the highway—as though it had torched itself in protest.

I was also acutely aware of my own insignificance as I began to grasp the sheer size of Bangkok. There are no official numbers of how many people live here, because at least 2 million come and go according to what's happening down on the farm. Once the rice is in, there's zip to do but watch it grow. Despite that, a population estimate of 11 million wouldn't be far out.

Even the first exchange of words in a new country is often retained quiet clearly. Flying into Sydney, Australia in the late seventies, I was asked by the immigration officer if I had a criminal record. I said, "I'm terribly sorry, I didn't know it was *necessary* anymore."

Often the image of a new country is usually formed by the traveller before arrival. For many, England evokes images of old castles, red telephone boxes, and eccentric ladies in tweed skirts and sensible shoes pottering about in cottage gardens and waving to the postman.

Spare us, per*lease*. It is not that these things can't be found, it's just that they are no longer a true reflection of Britain— any more than the Reichstag is a mirror of Germany, or the Taj Mahal is of India.

Yet Thailand should not decline its own reflection. All that the country holds dear is still here. But behind the saffron and the smile there is a different reality at work. It can, and often does, take the newcomer by surprise. Indeed, strangers who come here seem stunned on arrival, and comatosed on departure.

Before leaving London, a travel agent neglected to mention to a visitor that his planned visit to Bangkok would coincide with the wet season. A week after his arrival, his parents received an urgent telegram: "STREETS FULL OF WATER STOP PLEASE ADVISE STOP." His father replied, "THEN SWIM YOU PRAT STOP."

A Thai's image of England may be one of a landed gentry living in large country houses. But the reality is more of a stranded gentry whose sheltered lifestyle comes in the shape of a cardboard box under a railway bridge in South London.

The rich might control a country, but they rarely represent its true pulse.

Still, there's always amusement to be found in the contradiction. In London, Mrs. Simpson (Edward VII's mistress) once climbed into a taxi and said, "King's Cross, driver." He replied, "Very sorry to 'ear it madam."

When I arrived in Bangkok, I applied to a large school for a teaching job. I asked the headmaster, "How many people work here?"

"About half," he replied.

A good indication of a caring society can be found in its attitude to its elder citizens. Although it is changing, Thai society, along with most Asian countries, treats its elderly with respect. It's a family thing. In South London, however, an old age pensioner is frequently perceived as a slow-moving target.

Equally, the quality of a country can be measured by the manners its citizens display towards the visitor. A Thai friend reserved a table at a restaurant while staying in New York because he liked the sound of its name: GET FAT.

When he arrived, he realised the place was full of seasoned celebrities with serviceable smiles. It smelled of failure. The snooty *maitre d'* held up an imperious hand and asked, "Do you have a reservation?"

"Yes, several," he replied, "but I've decided to eat here anyway."

On landing in America, a customs officer asked Oscar Wilde if he had anything to declare. "Only my *genius*," he replied, famously.

What do we have to declare when arriving in *this* city? And perhaps more to the point, what do we do with it afterwards? Actually, don't tell me, I'd rather not know.

As a tourist's illusion, Bangkok is a disaster. But as a disaster, it's unique for the vibrant energy and self belief that it generates. At night, the blaze of light from this city could illuminate the heavens—and maybe those who watch us from far away may well believe it's a star in its own right. They wouldn't be far wrong.

Now *that* would make a lasting impression.

I Gave You the
Best Ears of My Life

When the first band I ever played in split up, I burst into tears, my mum sighed with relief, and my elder brother punched the air triumphantly and yelled, "YES! There *is* a God!" The neighbours gratefully took out their earplugs and opened the curtains for the first time in months.

Were we really that bad? No. We were infinitely worse. We called ourselves The Loud Rice. We certainly weren't edible, were hardly worth listening to, but far too loud to ignore. We only ever played one gig—as a support band for a puking punk outfit called Who Killed Bambi.

Our rehearsals consisted of four guys playing in a variety of tempos, in a mishmash of keys, at *very* competitive volumes. The result was a collision of odd rhythms, woeful tunes, random noises, and shameless mistakes. We didn't mind a bit because we already knew that if you played a bum note once, you could always play it again—and if anyone complained, you could say it was jazz.

I blame the whole thing on Jose Feliciano, who is blind. When I heard his "Light My Fire" for the first time, I sat with my mouth open and eyes shut, savouring the sound, and thought, "I want to do that. And what's more, I can see."

What started as a minor diversion was to become a wholesome obsession. A few years and several bands later, I woke up one morning on a lawn in Australia. My index finger was stuck in an empty bottle of Southern Comfort bourbon. I managed to make it to a phone—although with the bottle still attached it was very difficult to dial—and I told my mum, "I've recorded an original song and it's now number 29 on the Brisbane Independent Top 40 Chart."

"That's *marvelous* dear. Where's Brisbane?"

I played in an acid jazz outfit for a while, but it was challenging to play because none of us knew what acid jazz really *was*. Then the bass player helpfully suggested that we take some to find out. *Oooh* boy! From then on the music sounded perfect. The only problem was, we weren't playing it.

But I knew my rock 'n' roll days were over when I was halfway through singing a driving track called "Taking Care of Business" and I suddenly got a stitch in my side and had to lean against a stack of Marshall amps for the rest of the song.

So it was back to Feliciano, who I now realised could see much better than I ever would. His talent was in his feel for the music, not the notes on the page. A very important lesson. But trying to capture his loose, beautiful, seductive, Latino guitar style proved illusive—though I seem to have developed my own bastardised version of it over the years.

I never came to Bangkok to play music for a living. Nine years was enough already. In fact, to get here I sold my Ovation guitar to a Thai who had just sold his piano to get to where I was about leave. Coincidence? Not at all. Show me someone who believes in coincidence and I'll show you someone who hasn't been paying attention. Musical instruments have a mind of their own, and sooner or later the good ones always end up in the right hands. I've also learned to never underestimate God's sense of humour.

I've seen a lot of talented players in this town. I've also noticed a lot of untalented ones getting far more attention and money than the talented. A combination of looks, studio twiddling, video fiddling, kickbacks, and sex, can do wonders for a career.

There are also players here just going through the motions simply to survive. And believe me, there is nothing worse in the world for a musician than to be playing a song he doesn't like, to a crowd that isn't listening, for money that isn't worth it.

It's tricky to write objectively about music because it's such a subjective experience. Everyone hears it differently, especially the song you really like—and if there's one thing worse than your older brother's favourite CD, it's your younger brother's favourite CD.

Yet the direction of music seems to have changed, or rather, it has completely lost its way. To me, much of today's popular music sounds contrived, manufactured, and lacking in the one crucial element that gives music its power and elegance: soul.

Look at your average 'rock' star, either here or abroad. Far from being rebellious, these people are now essentially conservative, because they conform to what is *expected* of them. The rock scene has become a caricature of itself—the shaking hair, the run across the stage, the pouting lips, the come-hither look, the arrogant self-importance. Yawn.

Rock music has lost its appetite and courage for change, and now feeds on itself. It's all so predictable, and those who play it are going nowhere and taking us with them. To grow, rock has to take chances. And screaming louder and playing it faster won't work. It's been done already. And far better. Rock *does* have a history, and it *will* have a future; but if rock musicians won't take risks, then who the hell will?

Music's best qualities seem inextricably knotted to its gravest faults, for in the world of rock and pop we continually read of record crowds and the millions grossed, as if the T-shirt sales are more interesting and important than the actual performance—which is actually quite often the case.

As a result, many acts become so entrenched in the numbers that their reputation far outweighs anything as trivial as their actual achievements. They certainly don't help their cause when they then surround themselves with a tawdry entourage of the beautiful and vapid, and buy vast mansions from the very part of society their music was supposed to be railing against: the privileged.

Musical integrity is very important to dedicated musicians, but nothing beats record sales.

Moreover, the teenage years now seem to start at eight or nine in terms of entertainment tastes. The emotions are kicking in earlier. It's a huge audience, and to feed it, the bands are now younger—much younger. There have been a couple of them through Bangkok lately who didn't look old enough to be allowed into a supermarket, let alone a pub to play in.

There is music and there is music, and then there is muzak which is bad music on Prozac, and karaoke which is dead music on vodka. Who let these two ugly words into the language anyway? They should not be classed as entertainment, but used as weapons. Put the two words together and you get . . . prokazot—a double dose of aural pollution. A lethal combination. You could invade countries playing this shit—and win without firing a shot.

Humphrey Bogart once said, "You're not a star until they can spell your name in Karachi."

I have never fancied Karachi, but I did see the Rolling Stones' guitarist Keith Richards walk out of a shop in Rome when I was 16. Even then his face was deeply tanned and so cracked it looked like a turtle's scrotum. He looked magnificent.

I'd like to think my tastes in music are becoming more discerning, but I know I'm just getting older. I'd prefer to think it's a cocktail of the two. But I was very fortunate in having a friend who, although didn't play an instrument, had a vast knowledge of music—and taught me what a wide palette it covered. I remember being impressed, not merely by his love of music, but that he knew what was intrinsically good—and, more importantly, why.

His choice was as diverse as it was wise; from Wolfgang Mozart to heavy metal, from catchy pop melodies to the subtleties of jazz. And he was acutely aware of how different levels of music could move people. It was the beginning of a wonderful and ongoing education. He believed that for those who understood it, music was an emotional and intellectual odyssey. And I couldn't agree more. He once quipped, "The way I see it, one form of rap music is as unfortunate as another, and I have been told that Wagner's music is better than it sounds."

Ah well, each to his own. Indeed, this very Saturday night people will be watching, playing, listening to, dancing to, and making love to a thesaurus of sounds all over the planet—from Japanese Elvis impersonators in Las Vegas to Opera in Milan, and from cool jazz in Chicago to the dark satanic bars of South London where the line up at the Gabriel Rock an' Reggae Club will be The Cruising Mooses, followed by Zen Terrorists, Beware of the Dog, Sniper, Sack The Juggler, and, finally, Pimp.

And Jose? He's still as blind as a bat and can see further than ever. He will be playing this very evening at the Jazz Café in London, NW1.

Let the music play, but please remember the neighbours. OK, don't then. I never did.

Elvis Spotted in Hilltribes

I love chaos. It's the natural state of the universe, and that's probably why I continue to live here.

Thailand manages to reflect celestial engineering in its true form—which is random, curved, slightly ridiculous, and always behind schedule. Even the religion preaches that life is neither permanent nor real, and I couldn't agree more.

But we all need to step outside, and after the madness of *Songkran* and watching the rising pillars of the electric Lego train set—which will only *ever* carry people who don't own a car—it was time for a change of geography.

In search of some space, my first brush with northern culture was some graffiti over a trekking shop in Chiang Mai:

"ELVIS SPOTTED IN HILLTRIBES!"

Inside, an excited Japanese backpacker told me that he'd been in training for a particularly long trek in the hill country. "The last few weeks have been *hell*," he panted. "I've had to give up drinking *and* karaoke!"

Great. It convinced me to forego a forced march.

Anyhow, I hate trooping off in a gang, and I don't like rafts—too exposed and you end up eating people—so I rented a motorbike with the intention of heading into the mountains, which are not high, just steep and meaningful. So I signed the contract, which was oiled into my hands by a retired Englishman called Chris. It read,*"The business is over. I am appreciated and will cause no longer problems. Thank you."*

He wanted my passport, some money, my mother's maiden name, and a urine sample. The only people he conversed with were his clients, and, occasionally, the police. I liked him immediately.

The next morning at dawn, still awake and wobbling a bit—the local whiskey was so good it had gone down singing hymns—I did a final checklist of the bike, and a weird thought crossed my mind. What was Lee Harvey Oswald's shopping list on that fateful morning in Dallas?

Buy milk.

Pay gas bill.

Cat food.

Kill President.

Feed goldfish . . .

Sixty kilometres north of Chiang Mai you turn left if you want to reach Mae Hong Song, 1,739 curves away. Facing the west, mosquitoes of bird-like proportions were whizzing past me when I noticed the sign: "CHIANG MAI ADVENTIST SCHOOL, TURN UP HERE."

On impulse, I steered the bike down the muddy track, over a rickety bridge which I nearly fell off—in anticipation of a disaster, some small children squealed in delight—through a gate, and into the grounds of a boarding school.

The trimmed and tree-shaded playing fields, surrounded by colonial-style bungalows with laughter coming through the open windows, made me feel as though I was arriving at the school I was always *supposed* to go to, but somehow there'd been a terrible mistake.

I rode up to what I presumed was the office, and was greeted by the charming, softly-spoken headmaster. His smile was accompanied by a slightly raised left eyebrow as he took in the spectacle before him. Seriously disheveled, with two dead dragonflies embedded in my left cheek, I could hear him thinking, "Let me show you around, we don't often get people from another planet dropping in."

I asked to sit in on an English class. The girls blushed, the boys laughed. They were all bright-eyed, polite, and about as rarefied as the air. I spotted the guitar propped in the corner with strings that were last changed in 1963. As a gesture, I thought I'd give them a tune or two. The class clapped as I started to strum the barbed wire.

But the headmaster was way ahead of me. "Why don't you *teach* us one?"

Of course, but what? Think . . . think . . . Christian school . . . OK . . . OK. "Stand By Me."

I wrote it on the board, we all sang it together, and then the headmaster said, "Is there anything we can do for *you* Mista Lodga?"

Well yes, I thought. Can I stay for a decade? But it came out differently: "Thank you, but you've done more than enough."

Earthed by this dream, it was back to the road and the real chaos that is here to test us.

Still Waiting Sir

The slow train to the north could not begin without a long flight to the west. In between, the trip went below the earth—where the loudspeakers on Victoria Underground Station in London vibrated with accents from Barbados and Uttar Pradesh.

A perilously thin busker squeaks out a reedy tune on his flute that echoes along the toilet-tiled corridors. He's so pale he's almost transparent. I can imagine the scene at a hospital.

"He doesn't need an x-ray doctor, just hold him up to the light."

There's an air of menace on the crowded tube, and those who failed to get a seat, stand on the feet of those who did. Emerging from the Dickensian tunnels, another train rattles and rolls me towards Scotland. I walk to the refreshment bar and notice that a youth with Rastafarian hair has plonked his monster ghetto blaster on the table in front of two aged pensioners who are visibly withering under the sound.

At a brief station stop in Lancashire, I glance out of the window to see a dog peeing on the back wheel of a new car in a sale yard. On the windscreen the sign says, "Only £4,250. Won't last!" The dog was just confirming it.

I had come in search of a past that might give me a glimpse of the present—and, perhaps, the future. My old school. I am not one for sentiment, or even nostalgia come to think of it, but as I was visiting my ninety-year-old grandmother who lived close by—and who still drives faster than her age—I thought I'd go and have a peek.

Except it wasn't there. The boarding school's once elegant Victorian buildings and green playing fields had been replaced by ugly bungalows. I was at first mortified, then horrified; my past had been reduced to a housing estate.

When I had first arrived at this boarding school—which held to the "profound belief in the health-giving properties of sea air and mountain walks"—my parents were fussed over by the headmaster and his wife. I was seven years old and told to make myself "useful" in the library. But it had no science-fiction section and the dictionaries were too old to have any swear words. So, I spent the rest of the morning torturing woodlice in the arboretum with a magnifying glass. It was brilliant. After lunch, I was taken to see the animals on the school farm. Nothing died or got dangerous so it was boring. I clearly remember the first night. I was going to stay awake to see the school ghost, but a senior boy said it was a *girl*—so I didn't bother.

There will always be misconceptions about private boarding schools in England. Most boys who were sent away at an early age to these establishments during the fifties and sixties, were primarily from middle-class nuclear families. And, like most things nuclear, they had a tendency to blow apart. Either through death, divorce, or debt. There were nine boys in my class, and none of them had fathers. These preparatory schools—which took boys from aged six to 13— were to prepare them for public schools, which were, in fact, private. But that's another story.

But were we lashed into Latin and thrashed into breakfast?

No. But we were certainly pushed.

We were spotty kids learning dead languages, and what we ate often seemed *far* older. I will always remember the food simply because it was so unforgettable. For seven years it was basically thick splidge with added splat. The salads were always known as "Apartheid"—because there were several oddly-coloured ingredients living separate lives on the same plate.

We thought our headmaster was so old he ran on magic. But he was a handsome and dignified man who taught us arithmetic, algebra, and geometry—three subjects that I hated, was dismally bad at, and had entirely forgotten by the age of 14.

He once asked us in class, "Is man a risen ape or a fallen angel?" There was a deathly silence.

Then a tiny voice piped up from the of the back of the class: "A fallen ape."

Which sent us sniggering and pointing, and at which the headmaster yelled at us for both crimes. That brave but squeaky voice belonged to a boy called Carter, who went on to play professional Rugby League in Australia, which is, without doubt, the toughest contact sport on the planet. Even at 11, he knew exactly what the state of man was.

Yet the headmaster's intentions were of the highest order, and by the year I joined the school, he had begun to rely on his humanity rather than his position to get the best out of us—and the knowledge out of him.

Not surprisingly my first report read: "It's not that he can't, it's just that he won't."

The school was established in the late 1800s, and down in the local library I discovered some old records:

January 1872: "B. Smith well caned for carelessness, idleness, and general inattention."

December 1911: "Coughs etc and worse. School sounds like a dog kennel on moonlit night. Choir practice totally out of the question."

August 1957: Report: Morgan R. E. "He spends his life finding new ways to avoid success by setting himself low personal standards and then failing to achieve them."

In 1910, there were 60 boys registered at the school. By 1915, 26 had been killed in the First World War, their names carved into the stone walls of the exquisite church we trooped down to every Sunday in the town. School caps on, and hands out of pockets, we were the epitome of manners and discipline. The little old ladies in the seaside town always smiled with approval and referred to us as "those *nice* young men from Charney Hall."

So, not being able to find the school, I entered this spiritual nursery to hear the echoes of hymns sung long ago. And then I suddenly remembered one Christmas service. Some giggling had started on the front row, followed by a lot of nudging, and by the time it got my pew, the whispered message was: "David Coultard's got his dick out. Pass it on."

Our chaplain, who was so pious and thin we nicknamed him the "Skinned Guinea Pig," strongly believed in salvation, and was forever saying, "If ever you need me, just ring the chapel bell."

So we did. Frequently. Usually at about 3.30 a.m.

I reflected on the scant news of my old school mates. The sensible had married the daughters of rich farmers from the Yorkshire Dales and the Lake District—God's own country. One became a Professor of Metaphysics at Oxford University, and another was part of the 1982 Mt. Everest expedition. One had half his face blown off on Tumbledown Mountain in the Falkland Islands. Two fell to the dangerous spike of heroin—one got up, the other didn't. One went into a sodden and unforgiving jungle to look for diamonds, and ten years later I got a smudged card from Jeaneau in Alaska—where he was *now* looking for gold—which said, "It's as cold as a nun's bum up here." Well, he was in the school choir.

I actually met up with two old boys when I was 18. One went off to a Jimi Hendrix concert to "get experienced" and never came back. Another went off to Japan to "get perfect" and did. And you know what? He *was* perfect; horrifically, annoyingly perfect.

So we beat him up and told him to go and look for the guy who went to the concert. Now they are both missing.

And the lessons I learnt from those now dead masters?

Hold fast to what is good and true, guard what is beautiful, defend what is precious, master your craft, be loyal to your friends, guide and cherish the young, forget yourself, and remember others.

All noble values, but what I really remember is the day the headmaster told us he'd been to a land called Siam and had seen a ghost dissolve before his eyes.

Well, Sir, I'm still here, and still waiting for one to turn up—let alone disappear.

Oscar Bait

In the old Soviet Union there were two major newspapers. Both, naturally, were run by the Communist Party. One was called *Pravda* (The Truth), and the other, *Izvestsia* (The News). The joke on the street was that in *The News* there was no truth, and in *The Truth* there was no news. Sound familiar?

Don't worry: money and great prizes can be won from both paradox and hypocrisy.

Let's take the Spratly Islands. Why not? Everybody else wants to. It's all illegal and perfectly media-friendly. I tried to find them on a map the other day. It took a while. Oh, *there* they are. Believe me, they are nowhere *near* China.

However, China is very big, and the other contenders are very small.

Land claims originating from ancient maps, and from ancient peoples, have always been at best dubious, and at worst emotional. Result? Trouble—and a godsend to the legal business. World courts are used, expensive lawyers are hired, and the press presses.

And these days everyone is doing it: comfort women, Australian Aboriginals, and large ocean-going mammals are all putting in their claims. But just how far can you go back in time to claim injustice?

"Look, the ale was just kicking in. T'was sometime in 1066, methinks. We were just sitting peacefully on the beach at Hastings in England, enjoying our rat-on-a-stick picnic, and the next moment, these yobs with appalling haircuts hit the beach. Next thing we knew, our mate Harold had an arrow in his left eye and was screaming, "What French bastard threw *that...*?"

Result? Nine centuries of mutual insults hurled across the Channel, and I end up with a French surname.

So what are you doing on the weekend? Come on, let's *take* the Spratlys before anyone else does. What the hell! It'll soon be called the SPLATLYS before long anyway. We could pretend we were Greenpeace. No we couldn't. Forget that; I owe them money. You see, I cuffed one of their canvassers when he knocked on my door at 8 a.m. on a Sunday morning. He had long hair and I couldn't see his face. I thought he was a crazed Jehovah's Witness. Well, what would you have done?

Anyhow, Greenpeace are too politically correct, and they are never wrong. I'm neither of these things. So, what we *will* do is get smart and make a movie out of it as we invade.

In the immortal words of Carl Sagan: *"Come* with me."

Our picture opens on a turquoise sea. Sigourney Weaver, mohawked and saddled on a killer whale, called Kill Willy, emerges next to one pathetic hump of sand in the ocean upon which four Chinese soldiers are trying to erect a television aerial. She smirks, and they freak and jump into the water. She submerges, follows, and it's lunch for the whale.

It's disturbing, but timely. It's Oscar bait.

The camera then pans to another Chinese-occupied blip of land deeper into the Splatly claim. The commander, whose name is Wun Hung Bak, is a militant but well-meaning guy. But he has an evil streak owing to the loss of his left eye in a laboratory experiment in Shanghai in 1962. It is covered by a patch, ingeniously fashioned from the sloughed husk of a favourite tarantula. He has more hair in his ears than he does on his head.

To a hip-hop soundtrack, Sigourney emerges once more, erect on the whale. She is powerful. Wun Hung Bak wheels around and spots her with his good eye.

"Ah, so we meet again old friend, eh?"

He immediately launches himself into one of those ridiculous twenty-foot Kung Fu backward somersaults, and lands on his own sword at exactly the same place he started.

Sigourney is unmoved, but stiffens at the sight of the approaching ships.

Dramatic pan to Splatly panorama. Sigourney, using only a blowgun and a flare, takes out the entire Chinese deep-water navy. It's action. It's nineties. It's Eco-*Aliens* with a *Guerrillas in the Mist* twist.

Of course there'll be dolphin-related casualties and heavy gunfire, but it's topical. It's worth a fortune in baseball cap and T-Shirt contracts.

When the greenies arrive to congratulate her, she blows them away too, mouthing "Hippy wimps" as she slowly disappears beneath the waves.

Final scene. Sigourney, now peroxide blonde, triumphant, and astride her whale, cruises up the Chao Phraya river, where they receive a dramatic welcome just opposite the Oriental Hotel. There's thunderous applause, the teenagers scream, the paparazzi snap, and the whale blows water on cue. Sigourney holds her blowgun aloft in triumph.

But unknown to her and the crowd, a soured female English language teacher with distressed hair and a chin that shows no signs of coming out of the recession, edges towards the river with a sawn-off shotgun.

So how was your week?

Things Are Looking Up

It was the last day of term, 1971. My hair was a metre long. My tutor said, "You look like a damned Hottentot, and if you *insist* on becoming a musician, you'll probably marry one and end up living in an attic."

He was damn nearly right too. I *did* become a musician, *and* I married one, but we ended up living in the back of a car. But things are looking up. I now live between a slum and a disaster.

The slum is Klong Toey, and the disaster is Sukhumvit—a road which must surely hold more treasure beneath it than ancient Rome, for it's been excavated more times than most archaeological sites in history. The *soi* that connects these distinctive headlines is dishevelled, safe, and a cauldron of pleasing chaos.

The landscape around here changes every five minutes. Yet, some buildings, like the 17-floor concrete carcass next to my block, are in a permanent state of semi-abandonment. It took the locals two years to figure out firstly, what the hell it was, and secondly, how you get *into* the damn thing?

We asked the builders, who didn't know, who went to find the architects, who weren't even there. Then the builders asked us if we had any money . . .

Meanwhile, a Himalayan pile of refuse has risen over the year as the workers threw all their rubble, offal, and flotsams of snot over the wall. Around here, it's called recycling. We have inherited this squalid disgrace, which, naturally, is completely ignored by everyone except the rats—who think it's Las Vegas.

Wearing expensive shades, they lie on their backs, bloated with toxic waste, and look slightly guilty—as though astonished by their own abundance. Even the local dogs are embarrassed to be seen with them.

For the rest of us, it seems impractical to be uncivilised here, for there is an instinctive humanity in this hardworking neighbourhood—a vital philosophy of getting ahead and getting along. Relationships around here are amicable, but have purpose, and you'll find yourself pulped into fiction if you don't contribute one way or the other. Your money or your manners—preferably both—and we'll all get along just fine.

There are apartments full of foreigners living a cocktail of realities. There are thugs, drunks, losers, survivors, dreamers, talkers, and dot.com nancy boys. There are keen teachers, laid-back architects, suits, and those who appear to have spent the last seven nights outdoors in a wheelbarrow.

There are also those who come and go, speak fluent bratpack, and are so relaxed they can't even get out of their own way.

Last night I sat talking to two guys in one of the local bars. We were a confederacy of strangers. After drinking a *goon* of panther piss each, and about to start on the second *calabash* of palm wine, I discovered that one of them was making 250,000 baht a month as a salesman for computerised weaponry. The other guy, who had a face like a party balloon with a slow leak, didn't make any money at all— but just managed to maintain a ridiculous grin. Every time he wanted another drink, he simply yelled, "Nurse!" and they came running. What a brilliant idea.

He had all these pills in his shirt pocket. I asked him what they were for. "They make greyhounds incredibly happy for just a few moments," he explained.

Oh.

Suddenly, late last night, one pathetic lightbulb blinked on, then off, high up in the dormant concrete shell next door. Then early this morning, there was an excited shout from the street: "Hey! It's been called a hotel!"

Wow! Sometimes truth can come at you from completely the wrong direction. My *dear*, by lunch there'd even be talk of *guests* . . .

Right now, we're negotiating with Christo to come and wrap the refuse dump in white silk—as a sculpture, as a monument, as . . . as . . . as possibly another hotel.

But the squatters are not interested. A spokesgerm for the rats said they are demanding *pink* silk, fresh refuse, new Raybans, and a little female rat action after dark.

We're working on it.

Flood and Be Damned

I used to be in love with a beautiful Italian girl called Raffaella Mattioli. At 17 she was already cool and assured, while at 15 I was still decidedly juvenile and chaotic. Our respective families are of the opinion that only one of us has changed.

During the autumn term at the International School in Rome, she wore those kind of sweaters that made you pull your eyes over her wool. Her parents lived in an enclave of wealth and privilege, and, not unnaturally, security was tight.

Seeing her was a problem, and on many an evening I had to zip past the doorman and then *zap* past the Doberman. Her father was a consultant with the Venice Water Board, and his brief was simple: "Stop the city from sinking any further, by Friday if possible . . ."

Non problema.

He was away a lot and I found out later that he really had done some brilliant design work for saving Venice but, as a result, spent much time in Florence visiting his therapist—who was even more beautiful than the city. For an Italian, that's both normal and complimentary.

Over lunch on his vast terrace overlooking the Piazza di Spagna in Central Rome, he once told me that, "Water and blood are the great circulations of life."

As the wine flowed to background opera and his mind shifted down a gear, he told me of the "*Fontanieri*," whom I learned were the talented, medieval, hydraulic engineers whose liquid vocation was defined by changing stagnant water into flowing water; the pond into the fountain, mortality into vitality.

Ruins of the great aqueducts, arches, and reflecting basins that are littered throughout the Roman empire had survived "as a reminder" of the sheer imperial scale and esoteric language of water—its curve and flow, and the distance from its source—of which humans and animals are its grateful recipients.

One weekend he drove us to his villa at Caprarola, where his mistress lived in idle luxury surrounded by worthless sycophants. We travelled in his huge antique car.

"Ze engine is capable of 250 kilometres an hour," he said with a slow smile. "Unfortunately ze rest of ze car, is not."

All the way, Raffaella and I sneaked looks of *amore* in the back, while the Doberman drooled with evil intent over my left shoulder.

The grounds of the villa were stunning, and resembled a flowing chorus of water. The sides of the cascade that ran down the gardens were shaped as interlaced dolphins, to signify a safe and blessed journey across the waters of the world, and, often, from the mortal to the immortal realm.

He told me his work in Venice had always been stressful, but his depression was compounded one day when he spotted an overweight American tourist with a loud shirt and unforgiveable wife alight from a gondola at St. Mark's Square.

"He took off his gaudy sunglasses, looked around, and said dramatically, 'Don't . . . change . . . a . . . *thing*.'"

And he talked of Bangkok.

"It was once called the Venice of the East," he said. "But I believe it has changed."

Well yes, you could say that. But his love of the spiritual *mechanics* of water left a deep impression on me, and the question has to be asked:

What the hell happened here?

Will the waterways of Bangkok be vaguely remembered as some amphibian myth? And who was the group, sorry, *wok* of idiots who allowed the *klongs* to be filled in and filled up with foreign cars that have no flow, no movement, and no magic? Cars that are sold as an expression of individuality but aren't, because they all look exactly the same? Cars that should express wealth and position in society but don't, because a man in a rich car has to queue behind a man in a smoking wreck at the lights? It defeats the whole purpose.

You know, there *is* an answer. There *is* a way to restore the liquid grace to this city, so that it can once again be proud of its fluvial heritage—and through the mirrored windows of its buildings, reflect the water that made it so entrancing in the first place.

The answer? Flood it. And do it properly this time.

There is little doubt that nature wants to; it's been trying for ages. So let's help it. Unleash the river, clog the *klongs*, seal the drains, and let the waters flow through the arteries of the city like a vital sap.

Let it fill and two things will happen as a result: all the cars will be flushed into the Gulf, and the good citizens of Bangkok will once more be waterborne, just as the city intended them to be.

What? Too drastic?

Then think of something else then.

In the meantime, fly me to Italy and I'll get a second opinion—and maybe another chance to see Raffaella.

The Horse Yeller

The dawn brings rain. Mud everywhere. Rats and stench in the stables. It is my first visit to the Cumberland Riding School in Northern England—and it will be my last. I am 17, and I just *hate* horses.

And yet I know it makes no sense, because I come from a part of the country where wiry, weather-beaten vets can look into a horse's mouth and tell you its life history, while I couldn't even tell you what it had for breakfast.

A horse is led out from the stable and everything goes dark. Its massive chestnut frame eclipses the sun. It snorts, it shivers, and it has an erection the size of Italy. I show visible fear. Well, wouldn't you?

My head is hot and full of mistakes and questions like, Where's the ignition? How do you *stop* the thing? And, Why is it looking at me like that?

I am saddled up and reigned in. The instructor says, "You must show confidence, because riding a horse is just like life. Either you do it, or it does you." And with that, he slaps the beast's rump. It responds by accelerating to warp gallop in 4.3 seconds. Show confidence indeed. Where's the damn hand-brake? Where is this thing taking me anyway?

I only spoke to one other person that morning—while maintaining a manic and anxious conversation with myself the entire time. Another rider, a professional of course, waved in greeting from across a field as we flew past. "Out for a ride are we?" he shouted cheerfully.

"No! Being *taken* for one! Aaaaggghhh . . . ," I yelled back, as the horse plunged into some impenetrable woodland at a wicked rate.

In 1927, General Sir Raleigh Egerton wrote: "I consider that the horse has a humanising effect on men, and the longer we can keep horses for artillery and cavalry the better it will be for the British army, because thereby you keep up the high standard of intelligence in the man from his association with the horse."

An excellent point, but it wasn't helping me—and it didn't do much for King Richard III either, come to think of it. Only an *English* king would scream, "A horse, a horse, my kingdom for a horse!"

You wouldn't find any respectable *Mongolian* warlord swapping his kingdom for a lousy nag. No sir, he'd just *take* your horse, and quite probably your kingdom, your best women, and your finest Scotch as well. Then he'd kill you.

To warlords, the horse was cheap, dispensable, and disposable—yet still rated higher than people for its usefulness.

The cavalry in Genghis Khan's army had five spare horses *each*. These animals were short, muscular, and very, very fast. They weren't just horses, they were Mongolia's answer to the Exocet missile; whip, gallop, and *zap*!

Khan's horsemen were particularly adept at shooting targets to the rear as they flashed past—and each rider carried an arsenal of different arrowheads. Some were solely for killing, while others were designed to give a terrifying whistle which could also take half your face off. A whistle-while-you-maim arrowhead. They could unleash six arrows a minute, and Khan's armies were huge—usually numbering around 80,000 at any one time. So, wait a second; that's 6 x 80,000 a minute, which equals, er . . . a whole *orchestra* of carnage—humming, whistling, and deadly .

Each man carried: a bow made of wood, sinew, and horn; up to three quivers of arrows; a lance with a vicious hook and snare; a sabre; and a dagger strapped to his left arm. Small squares of iron were sewn into the lining of his boots to protect his calves, and to give maximum force when he ran out of weapons and had to resort to, well, putting the boot in.

This gruesome cavalry decimated the once elegant city of Herat in Western Afghanistan, over a thousand years ago. In the years that followed, old men could still be found in lonely, dusty alleys shaking their heads slowly and muttering to no one in particular, "He left nine . . . just *nine* of us."

The annual *gorugen*, or great hunt, became the basic training for Khan's recruits. Encircling animals in a given area, the horsemen would close in. Each rider was allotted one arrow. Failure to kill met with ridicule. There was none of this, "Now, Gorzak Bulba, let's see you give the appropriate hand-signals, while maintaining proper control of the animal." No. To pass the test, you had to *kill* something. Cool. Mongolian cool.

Assuming we have all lived past lives—and I do—no matter how hard I try, every time I bring up the file named "Horse," there is nothing. No memory, no association. Zilch.

Anyhow, I'm not sure I even *want* to know what I did in my previous lives. For a start, I'm still here. Which means I keep getting sent back. Which means they can't have been all that useful or redeeming.

But I do have a distinct feeling of *déjà vu* whenever I dream of Khan's great armies. I reckon I was in his artillery battery. Nothing flash, mind you. In current parlance, the position would be the equivalent of a trash can attendant on a US aircraft carrier. I don't think we cared much, as I have a strong suspicion that men who were in artillery were an unruly mob, and were left pretty much to their own devices—or just vices. We did the dirty work—like catapulting disease-ridden corpses over the walls of besieged cities in countries whose names were always preceded by the word "Outer."

I seem to recall the job was actually a promotion. The wages were bad, the hours were long, and the smell was indescribable. But we got to meet plenty of women—some of whom were actually catapulted back over the city walls. Divorce, medieval style.

The horse at war. The horse at play. In 1930, a captain in the British army quipped, "The tank would never replace the horse until a sporting use could be made for it." Good point, because people have being having a ball on horseback for centuries.

Remember the *quintain*? Perhaps not. But surely you've heard of the *gibbet*? No? Ah . . .

OK. A quintain is a wooden construction that looks exactly like a gibbet, which was a simple wooden frame that was used to hang people from. It could once be found on nearly every village common in England's green and pleasant land.

Later, the gibbet was refined into the quintain, which, instead of having a noose at one end, now dangled a heavy sack full of wet horse dung. It's purpose was fun and challenge.

The idea was that the horse rider, armed with a long stave, would come at the thing at full gallop and try and hit the sack, making sure he ducked or accelerated away fast enough before the bag of dung spun viciously around and knocked him senseless to the ground.

Good fun to play and great fun to watch—especially after 12 pints of 14th century English Dogbolter home-brewed beer inside you.

What's more, nobody whispered to horses in the middle ages.

You've Either
Got it or You Ain't

The sign on the notice board at the Villa Supermarket said it all: Lovely condo for rent. 3 bdrms., nice lounge, gdn., kitch., fax, maid available, delightful, convenient [she sounded perfect!], on Sukhumvit. Only Bt85,000 mth., 3 mths deposit.

Eighty-five thousand baht a month? For rent? You could buy Zambia for that. And half of Russia with the deposit. Who's paying this kind of money? And why? And more to the point, why don't they give *me* some of it?

There's nothing like money for separating people. Like it or not, cash defines us. Leave your hut in this city and your wallet starts to glow. Your status as a foreigner has nothing to do with how well you speak the language or understand the culture.

Sorry about that. It's money that establishes position, earns respect, and issues its own passport to the lifestyles of the rich and shameless. Show enough and suddenly everyone is listening. Spend enough and you have new-found friends—or rather, they have found you. No one cares if you're from Chad or Chicago.

In Bangkok there are several classes divided by the "Bahtability Factor." The parameters of the society range from the cloud-piercing penthouse class on Sukhumvit, where the monthly income hovers between 200,000 baht and none of your damn business (and they don't even *pay* the rent), to the desperately-seeking-a-squat-class off Bang-lampoo, where the inhabitants use a pig on a string as an air freshener, and sleep on designer straw. They stagger around half sober, narcotically confused, with eccentric hairstyles that have to be ironed into submission, and survive on a princely income of 19 baht a month—which has either been borrowed, or stolen. Quite possibly from you.

To qualify for the middle-class you need around 80,000 baht a month. This strata includes insurance men, club owners, advertising wallahs, architects, and computer nerds who wear their glasses upside down, eat floppy discs for breakfast, and whose idea of a good night out is to stay in and abuse the mouse. It's a notch up from "bus conscious-ness," but a floor down from a really good view.

For journalists and teachers, musicians and writers, and those with long and winding CVs ("Hey man, wanna buy a degree?"), the income tends to be flexible—let's say from zero to 50,000 baht a month. It's more of a roller-coaster existence than a defined class. Try not to look down if you can help it, because there is no safety net—only the bus and the potential to look for love in all the wrong places. Definitely character revealing though.

I come from a culture where you are still judged—and thereby classed—by the kind of car you have parked in your driveway. Make? Datsun Insult. Colour? Um . . . , rust with flaky bits.

In Thai society, this takes on even greater significance. As long as the brand-new, teal-green, top-of-the-line Mer-cedes is gleaming in the sunlight, it doesn't matter that 19 family members have lived in one room above the shop-front, and granny has been chained to the sewing machine for the last two years to pay for it.

The face that you've gained now places you in the class that you wanted. You've arrived.

Or have you? Is it *really* the toys you can afford that promote you to prominence?

Being a foreigner has different advantages. Having no face, we have no face to lose, which means you've just saved 4 million baht on a car that never gets out of second gear—and, suddenly, you're elevated into a position of choice.

Just don't forget to unchain granny.

All right, don't bother then.

Another bonus is that because Bangkok is a multi-levelled society—faceless but with attitude—you can actually learn to cruise the classes to discover how everybody else lives. It doesn't even take money. It just takes a little practice, discrete charm, and blatant lying.

A friend of mine was sitting in his usual dishevelled splendour in the riverside restaurant at the Oriental Hotel. After devouring a large meal and sinking a good bottle of wine, he whispered to the man at the next table that he hadn't got any money. The man's expression quickly changed from surprise to concern, and then he said, "Don't worry, I'm an American." And immediately paid the bill. Don't you just love Americans?

I'm certainly not advocating this audacious scam. The real point is that it takes a certain sense of class, however nefarious, to pull it off.

Applying for well-paid jobs that you are not qualified to do is also worth a try in the class-hopping game. Borrow clothes and adjust your resume accordingly. But not too much, otherwise people might get suspicious.

"Your credentials are very impressive Mr. Prat, but where exactly *is* the Mahatma Gandhi Institute for Advanced Switch-Gear Technology and Shorthand Typing?"

But then this city can make you do crazy things. It's forever changing your plans. It can lull you into a sweet sense of belonging, and then confront you with the fact that life is played but once—why waste it somewhere else?

So, whether you're perched so far up in the charged atmosphere of serious income to give a damn, or, alternatively, you live in a box underneath the stairs at the Texas Lonestar in Washington Square, homeless, phoneless, and hopeless, don't worry—because money has actually got nothing to do with it.

Personally, I've often found that those who have the most money are eminently capable of displaying the least class. In fact, the rich are boring company. Why? Well, because they *are* rich means they don't have to fight anymore, and if you don't have to fight, you don't have any fire, and if you don't have any fire, you don't have any passion. Result? Boring.

And yet arrogance and ignorance are not confined to those with an overdraft. And a high income does *not* guarantee good taste.

Because class is not something that can be bought.

It is really defined by character, and expressed through style. To be a courtesan of good taste costs nothing, and as Marilyn Monroe once admirably remarked:

"Class? Why, honey, you've either got it or you ain't."

Lead Us Not into Temptation

I received a birthday card from my brother last week. It was three months late, which is normal for him, and the tasteful illustration pictured that gothic horror shop of England, the bloody Tower of London. On it he wrote, "Wish you were here."

He's always been a man of words—not many, but always meaningful. Speaking of words, I was leaning against the wall of smog the other day, nonchalantly filing my talons, when I realised how little of the Thai language I have truly learned since my arrival.

Yesterday, when I asked someone for a light, I was really asking them to set me on fire. Then last night, I asked the manageress of my apartment block to give me an early alarm call—yet apparently she understood that I wanted her to wash me at 6 a.m. With a surprised look and a raised eyebrow she was evidently caught between saying, "How *dare* you and how much?"

Whatever, it was another social blunder.

Besides language, there is the question of alcohol.

Do foreigners tend to drink more in Bangkok?

Yes.

Do foreigners really have a problem with the stuff?

Of course they do.

What is it?

The expense.

Drinking alters not merely our state of mind, but also the fate of nations. It kills far more people than heroin, and promotes more benevolence than religion. Above all, being awash makes reality tolerable, even enjoyable—and don't panic, it's organic.

I have a friend who is tiny and remarkable, and was formerly addicted to self-help groups. He has a face like a surprised potato. His life in Bangkok is one long happy hour, and his favourite dish is the ashtray. He is permanently at that stage where he is unable to recognise anything unless it wanders directly into view. Even then, shapes and memories are blurred. He asked me, "Wot's dish Russhun brandy made of?"

"It's made of criminals," I replied, and asked him if there was anything he wanted.

"Yesh, an ecstatic hour."

He lives in an apartment which has all the comforts of a World War II submarine with a leak—and because his numbers are dazed, his days are numbered.

Yet he can still raise a finger to the health nuts.

"*Jogging*?" he snorts. "*Yogurt*? *Jogging* on yogurt? Yuck. It sounds like luggering. Listen, the longest-living people on this planet come from the Carpathian mountains. They make love a great deal, which is the foremost circulatory exercise there is. They smoke disgusting cigarettes made of pig dung that clog the arteries, and then drink copious amounts of vodka to open them. It's a balanced diet."

His mother, who was a well-known poet and a drunk, once brilliantly remarked, "I'm too important to be famous," and promptly fell over.

Their family motto was, "Lead us not into temptation, just tell us where it is and we'll find it."

Indeed. The Welsh poet, Dylan Thomas proclaimed with noble resonance, "Love the words, love the words." He also loved his alcohol too—and it killed him.

Humanity has advanced, when it has advanced, not because it has been sober, responsible, and cautious, but because it has been playful, rebellious, and immature. Creation is not yet complete, and being merely human, or at least apes with briefcases, we are allowed to make mistakes. The hitch is responsibility and self-discipline—words which may seem out of place in this city where a stop sign is seen as a suggestion.

Yet when your liver is on incipient meltdown and screaming for mercy, and your life becomes so messy that you can't even organise a bucket in a monsoon, you are left with two choices. You can either retire to a monastery and read *The Tibetan Book on 101 Ways to Avoid Reincarnation*, or you can get Ray, a gay bartender, to whip-up a cocktail in the cold light of an empty glass.

As they say around here: "Up to you."

Love and Illusion

The Hindi word for illusion is *maya*. The English word for illusion is love. I have proof.

An Indian friend of mine in London was completely gaga over a girl in his office. He sent her enormous Valentine cards which he signed, "Your Baby Bhagwan." He sent her flowers and chocolates—which would arrive at the office in huge wicker baskets with frills and bows—and on one occasion, a live puppy.

He was dying of love while she was dying of embarrassment. But he persisted and she relented, and he stretch-limoed her to a series of Punjabi hotspots all over town. One night, they were spotted smooching in the Boob-Ooze Club in Soho, and a week later she moved into his flat, which was full of idols, incense, and questionable herbs.

A year later, he discovered she was having an affair with Prendergast from the purchasing department. My Indian friend was heartbroken, soul-beaten, deflated, morose, and then couldn't decide *how* he felt. But finally he settled on revenge. He nailed a poster of his cheating girlfriend's face on trees all around his neigbourhood bearing the caption:

"HAVE YOU SEEN THIS DOG?"

She subsequently went around her forest of humiliation ripping them down, and then decided to ring the immigration department.

The last I heard of him, he was back in Delhi and his parents had him engaged to a Gujurati girl, aged eight.

Love, *maya*, all is illusion.

It is said that bookshops have romantic potential. So I got a job in one. The work was fun, the wages were hilarious. I was told that the customer is always right. So I asked the manager, "If we can't smack the children, can we at *least* belt the parents?"

No, I certainly could not.

Oh.

So I used to lie in wait by the romantic airport novels for single ladies. They all eyed me suspiciously, and one complained to the manager that a pervert was lurking near the Mills and Boon stand.

Absolute *maya*, madam. It's an illusion, it wasn't me.

But I soon discovered that the only love to be found in a bookshop was not under the covers, but between them.

According to one major bookseller, humanity has varied reasons to frequent these establishments.

A survey revealed that:

20% are waiting for someone,

3% are *hiding* from someone,

20% are waiting for it to stop raining,

5% are lost,

10% are thinking about stealing a book,

10% are looking in awe at the artwork on the covers,

another 15% are looking in awe at the *prices* on the covers,

10% are looking for girls,

and 1% are looking at the people who are looking for girls—which leaves the princely total of 7% who might actually get around to buying a book.

An intellectually undernourished actor from Hollywood once said something quite perceptive: "Chasing women is fine and fun, but it's when you actually *catch* one that the problems start."

His fear was not of commitment, but of entrapment. He may be on to something there, but then he's divorced and dead—which proves that even mortality is *maya*.

On Valentine's Day last year, I was with a bunch of friends at a restaurant on Silom. The air was heavy with mashed, karaoked ballads that should only be let out with a license very quietly on Valentine's Day, but which are played incessantly all night long and all year round in this city.

Everyone in the room had a mobile phone which they shouted into periodically—probably at each other. The beautiful girl from next door, who has a body that pops thermometers, was sitting next to her new boyfriend from Noo Yawk.

"You'll like this guy," she said. "He's a bastard's bastard."

To me he was just another ego in a wig. They were soon entwined and valentined at the table, and I was sitting on the other side of her—ignored and desperate. He swaggered to the microphone and from the jungle of my lungs I blurted out to her, "Can I marry your hair?"

She gave me that, did-you-just-say-something look, as the words hung in the lucent air . . .

The Noo Yawker was still murdering "My Way" when I started drinking the ashtray.

Some enchanted evening. Thank God all is *maya*.

Across the Baize

I found the entrance by mistake. That could well have been the intention because, although the arrangement seemed secure, the address was decidedly vague—hidden, as it was, amid a dark labyrinth of back sois that gurgled with mischief and neon glitz.

Nevertheless, I was greeted by a smiling dwarf with a metal leg, who pushed aside a heavy red drape, and led me along a piss-stained corridor.

Venue? Bangkok snooker club. Time? About 9.30 p.m. Temperature? Rising. Corruption? About 80 per cent.

Welcome to the *real* world of snooker. A world of dedicated players who seek gratification through the game, and frequently find it by using their skills to separate you from your money, if you don't keep your eye on the ball. Literally.

It's also illegal. Which doubles the fun, and, quite often, the stakes.

This is a world of hustle, challenge, and addiction. Although the atmosphere appears to be laid-back and fairly congenial, it's just a front for strangers with awkward questions.

On each of the 15 full-size tables there is a game in progress, and, therefore, money on the outcome. There is little chat because someone has to win, and someone has to lose between the fangs and claws of instant happiness.

Thailand is a nation of game players who fool with the rules to suit the occasion. Golf is perfect for deal making and power broking—which is why caddies know more about what's going on here than anyone else. When a bigwig takes 20 minutes over a putt on the 18th hole, it's not that he's hoping to emulate Tiger Woods, it's because there's 100,000 baht and an apartment block in Nong Khai riding on the outcome.

So it is with snooker. Inter-club tournaments involving high calibre players can attract enough money to buy, well, a golf course. Like most imports, snooker has been dramatically tweaked and honed to suit the culture. The table, equipment, and basic professional rules may be standard, but the Thais have developed their own variations of the game, with names like "Electricity," "Striped Ghost," and "Russian Snooker." The difference being, they make the games much faster, more exciting, and completely unpredictable. They also ensure a result that lines the pocket of the player, the opponent, and the punter. In essence, the match is gambled on as it *goes* along. Indeed, there are games within games. Most variations use only six red balls, but for some, even that takes too long. Hey, why not bet on one ball? And why not bet on one ball going into *that* pocket? Here's 1,000 baht if you sink the pink in the top left. You're on.

Pro snooker began to make its presence felt in Thailand when Barry Hearn brought Steve Davis and a couple of his stablemates to play an exhibition match here in the mid-eighties—which coincided with the rise of Thai cuesman, James Wattana.

Prior to this, there were probably fewer than thirty snooker parlours in Bangkok, all of which could only be described as lacking in style—not to mention air-conditioning, a decent table, and a reasonable chance of getting out alive. Fees were 4 baht a game, and you left your wife or girlfriend at home. Definitely a boy's night out.

Today, snooker halls can be found on every major thoroughfare, and there are plenty more tucked away like this one, whose name I cannot reveal because I am quite attracted to life. Many clubs are still dingy dives full of hoods and hitmen—but downtown and upmarket the newer clubs boast bars, carpets, cable TV, and private rooms along with attractive female staff who set the tables, keep the score, and retrieve the balls. (No. Don't even *think* about it.) Fees are now charged by the hour, and range from 90 to 550 baht. Upcountry, a snooker table can be found in almost every village headman's front yard.

However, if you're thinking of starting your own club, I suggest you pour a large Scotch and sit down. For starters, you will have to obtain a license—which comes in at around half a million baht—to be paid to certain gentlemen who officially don't earn much, but seem to own an incredible amount. Secondly, you'll need a "stable" of at least ten top players who will have to be taken care of. The average parlour has 12 full-size tables, each costing around 400,000 baht. You'll require staff that are courteous, hard-working, discrete, and, preferably, armed.

You'll also need balls. They are a necessity in this game.

Shall I pour you another, or have you decided on a flower shop instead?

But if you are still determined to "play" in this snooker business, then you had better start watching the players who will make it pay for you. They fall into several categories, and, like any sport, there are very few of the very best—the cream of which are currently led by James Wattana.

This elite is followed by the "A" class, who are well-known on the circuit and regularly make a century break.

Bets placed on these guys measure in the hundreds of thousands per game, with each player receiving a percentage. Many of these top rankers belong to a stable and live above the parlour rent-free. They are "owned," nurtured, and contracted by the club, and—just like prize stallions—are extremely valuable.

The "B" class are occasional century breakers, are still in touch with the top talent, and the punters are very much in touch with *them.*

"C" class players frequently make half-century breaks and are rising through the ranks, whereas the "D" class potter sometimes makes a good break, and the "E" class loser is going to take a century just to make one.

And then there are the hustlers. The classic snooker shark has a vague manner that conceals a very shrewd judgement. He's a loner who consciously plays down his talent. He'll enter a club in another part of town, saunter up to the *dais*— a raised area with two tables that are strictly for those with talent or money to burn—and suggest a game. Losing a few "small change" encounters to lay the trap, he'll then begin to obliterate the opposition, pocket the "serious money" and move on. He takes great care *not* to build a reputation, and harbours no desire to turn pro. Hugging the shadows and covering a wide area, he does very nicely indeed.

The "odds" players are the hustlers who frequent the clubs but don't play—preferring to study the form of those who do. They bet on the odds as to whether a player will pot a certain ball in a designated pocket or not. Wandering from table to table all day, they are practically part of the furniture, such as it is. They only drink water and don't always have their own teeth—but to these guys, it's not the game, it's the outcome. They figure on about 500 baht a day. That's 15,000 baht a month.

But to the true snooker addict, both the game and the outcome are of equal importance. A double rush. It could almost be called a "respectable" addiction, but it isn't. The typical snooker junkie is over 25 years old, unemployed, or a sales representative. He plays every day, usually from around 5 pm until the witching hour, while the true extremist thinks nothing of playing 40 hours straight. They neither eat nor drink on the short haul sessions because it dulls the focus. These addicts are open about their addiction. Many are married, and the wives don't seem too upset either—at least they know where their husbands *are*. Nonetheless, a mobile phone is *de rigeur*.

Finally, there are those players who love the game but play it badly. Let's call them "oddballs." They lose enormous amounts of money but they don't care—as they are masters at playing other games that they don't enjoy as much, but which earn them a fortune. Stocks, bonds, logs, girls, gems, opium. Whatever.

My snooker "contact" here is an oddball. He's a wealthy, elegant man with a brain the size of a small planet, who's hopelessly devoted to the game, and who loses far more than he wins. He wears black gloves to protect his hands from calluses, and he owns the most beautiful custom-made cue I've ever seen. It's a precision instrument, a work of art that's balanced and weighted to perfection, and comes with a double extension that makes "the rest" redundant. He has a special briefcase in which he carries his balls, cue tips, chopsticks, and chalk. Very OO7.

He can't remember when he last saw daylight, and asked me to describe it to him. I tried really hard, but I couldn't remember either.

He grinned at me and said, "I'll give you 300 baht if you sink the black in the centre pocket."

Click . . . missed by a mile.

Another game perhaps?

Absolutely.

All Aboard
the Feral Express

Sir Winston Churchill, that well-known, American-born conservative, once defined a fanatic as someone who can't change his mind and won't change the subject. If that definition is true, then we're surrounded by them—and probably doomed.

On my last journey to Malaysia on the "Disoriented Express," the train was seething with extremists and crammed with refugees fleeing from reason. I had a bunk in a carriage of anarchy.

The first guy introduced himself by interrupting. His brain was as frayed as his jeans. He wasn't a passenger on a train, he was a hippy on a mission. By the time the train had crossed the Chao Phraya and turned south, he had already insulted everyone he needed to. The possibility of a conversation never stood a chance as he ranted and sprayed his redundant philosophy in everyone's face.

"Give everyone forty acres and a mule," he splurted. "It's the only way to save the planet. By the way, have you got any ecstasy?"

He was from California. He had lost his mind and was losing his hair. I decided that he wasn't real, he was just a trick of the light.

"How long have you been in Thailand?" I managed to ask.

"I don't know. I woke up here."

And he staggered off, deaf to the language and blind to the culture.

The three spivs from Pattaya who held court in the restaurant car were large, friendly, and, mercifully, unarmed. They were tanned and tough, drank the train dry, and ate nails for breakfast. Naturally, they knew everyone who knew anything. They had stories, connections, inside information; they had everything covered. They winked at each other in conspiracy. I felt that gorillas would purr at their approach. They welcomed me. I read the menu—which was three pages of pure fiction—and sat back and listened.

They had a novel way of securing superior accommodation. They would check into a room and set fire to it. Then they would spray the room with foam, ring the manager, and pretend that they had saved the hotel from a devastating blaze. Naturally, they were upgraded to the best suite—free of charge. Drinks on the house.

"Works every time my son . . ."

I liked them, but then I'm easily led astray.

And then there was the depressed New Zealander. He used to be a policeman, he said, from Waputo or Wanatoke, or someplace.

I've always thought that a desire to join the police should be grounds for not being allowed to—even among a nation of sheep. Anyhow, he had come to Thailand to teach. It depressed him. He'd had four motorcycle accidents in three months, he didn't like the food, it was too hot, and he felt that everyone was trying to rip him off.

For a while, I was sympathetic, and then I realised that this guy *enjoyed* being depressed. He was hooked into the victim game. He had no curiosity. He didn't talk, he droned. He had the charisma of a peanut. He was a fanatic for failure.

"Have you tried alcohol?" I suggested brightly.

"Makes me sick," he moaned.

I may have invented a new word: Miserabalist.

The fanatics will not be budged. Their minds are set like concrete. They could never be accused of having a split personality, for there is no personality to split. They never ask questions. From Anchorage to Amsterdam, the fanatic is ignorant of geography, and the earth hums with the hustle of persuasion.

In a sweating alley in Georgetown, Penang, I shared a bowl of bobbing amoebas—that looked suspiciously like whales eyeballs—with an Italian guy who had just spent time in a neighbouring country where "Murder is regarded as a legitimate means of career advancement."

The country was run with refined menace by men who told the indigenous people, "Look, either the borders move, or you do. Got it?"

I looked up from the fishy gruel to see smoke rising from a hotel in the distance, and thought, "Ah, the boys have checked in."

I relaxed. Everything was functioning normally.

Australia: Top
Breeders Recommend it

Is your teenage son in Thailand in need of overseas experience—for an overdue dose of reality—but money's too tight too mention? No problem. All it requires is distance and foreign soil.

Instead of spending vast amounts sending him to the Royal Oxford King's College of Benson's Basic English, send him to Australia—to a farm. There are only two conditions. He must be over 15, and in acute danger of being pampered at home. Rewards? The chance to learn two languages for the price of none, and a whole lot more. A brief language test maybe necessary . . .

"Arzzit garn Gazz?"

"No wuckin' furries Wayne."

"Surf's poundin' man."

"Unreal! Goin'?'"

"Oath! Fangin' the ute right now!"

You have two minutes to translate. No conferring.

In Australia, farms are called "stations" and they can be big. Very big. I worked on one that was almost the size of Belgium—and there are plenty as large as Bali. The countryside is known as the "bush." Beyond that it's called the "outback." Any further and you have 24 hours to live. Maybe.

In England a cow needs a square acre of grass to be useful. In Northern Australia it needs 25 square kilometres to *survive*. Many cattle have never seen a human being until they are mustered. They then have to be tagged, injected, de-horned, and castrated. It's similar to wrestling with a small tank. It was my first job on my first day.

The next morning, I learned how to drive a trail-bike before breakfast, and how to use dynamite by lunch. I was told my third day would be light: a little sheep shearing. "Only about 80,000," said my boss. "Coupla days, max."

The real Australia is an initiation to a reality the spoilt have never known. It is not a place for wimps, but it should be.

In vast areas, Australia is a primitive place, shorn of trimmings and ornament. In Western Australia alone, you can fit Japan once and Texas twice—comfortably. It is pristine, beautiful, and hostile. It can be crude and monotonous, but it is always vigorous and honest.

In the outback, only the dawn can nudge the frozen blanket that covers the desert. From the east comes light, from the sun comes heat—baking and penetrative. By noon, horizons blur, mirages shimmer, and the light blinds like ice in the ferocious glare and heavy silence. Wild animals find shade, wish they had Raybans, and hope to come back in their next life as tourists. Meanwhile, the afternoons melt into a yawning waste of heat rising from an ancient and empty landscape. The governance of sand.

Nightfall unrolls a celestial map literally stacked with stars, while beneath it, the silvery landscape swings to the sounds of rutting wildlife.

This is a continent forged by fire, flood, and drought. Its largely unfished southern seas are enriched by the nutrients from Antarctic currents, where some fish are rumoured to be very, very old. Some of these creatures have been swimming since Captain Cook arrived 221 years ago. I've neither eaten, nor been eaten *by* one—but have no trouble believing they are there.

Back in the outback, cuisine is the art of deception. The rest is just elbow grease and heating. Feeling peckish and eight days walk from the nearest pizza? Easy.

First, catch lunch. Then follow the local recipe. For cockatoo soup: Kill bird when it is not looking; take one large pan and fill with water; place rock in bottom of pan and boil; add dead bird; simmer for two days; when cockatoo is cooked, chuck it away and eat the rock.

It is true that outback farms can be lonely places. Where I worked, the nearest McDonald's was ninety kilometres away—and that wasn't the fast food joint, it was the name of the neighbour.

Yet the interior is not without entertainment. You will hear the occasional "ping" of a rifle bullet hitting road signs that declare, "KANGAROOS NEXT 1,000 KM." There's the monthly visit from the 97-kilogramme Avon lady wearing her entire range of products on her face, and there's even some discreet smuggling in tractor magazines. A three-day drive to the nearest car wash is an exciting night out. Indeed, many Australians were conceived in one. Afterwards, they may spend a pleasant evening drinking in the Spitting Punk—a traditional pub—catching up with the local papers that scream headlines like, "MAN MUGGED BY WOMBAT, AGAIN."

Yes, but what about *that* woman? Relax. Pauline Hanson is not a person, she is a catchphrase that accuses the mouth that utters it. She's right about Australians being racist though—simply because there isn't a country on the planet that isn't. But she's wrong about who the Australians are racist towards. It's not the Asians they don't like. It's the *English*.

And why? Because we invented them. The country was founded by people we didn't want, who were sent to a place they'd never heard of. For a while, its inhabitants couldn't belch without cursing the English. Quite right too. They landed with few tools and a bad attitude, yet the first house ever built in Sydney looked quite impressive—until someone leaned against it.

Once these reluctant pioneers realised it was a one-way ticket, and had experienced several defining historical moments, they became Australians—irreverent, humorous, brave, inventive, and patient; a nation of individuals, and one of the most easy-going peoples on earth. I liked them so much, I married one.

But let me assure every Asian student, businessman, or visitor, that I have experienced, and seen other Englishmen receive, far more abuse than any Asian. After I had been called a "Bloody Pom" for the 15,911th time, an Australian friend finally informed me that they only really abuse the people they *like*. Well, what a relief that was.

Australia is now a modern place, but still in search of a culture. It's also a place where PC used to mean a postcard.

But is it seductive?

Yes, deliciously so.

Is it corrupt?

Your son will feel right at home.

What about gambling? Well, in Britain, lottery tickets are not sold in betting shops because it might encourage wider gambling. In Hong Kong, lottery tickets are sold only in betting shops to *discourage* wider gambling.

In Australia you can gamble wherever the hell you like.

Funny people, legislators. Great place, Australia.

But be warned. Your son may end up being homesick for a country he doesn't even come from.

Veni, Vidi, Versace

I have this weird theory that Rome and Bangkok were originally twin cities, but somehow got separated at birth. Ridiculous? Maybe. Checked the weather lately? Perhaps you should. The wet season is sending thunderous e-mails every day with its awesome build-up of power that quickly engulfs the city. And as the light fades, the city broods in the heavy silence of anticipation.

It's a Biblical moment, a Hollywood minute—as the citizens await the deluge. It feels as though someone, somewhere, is about to be crucified.

Bangkok, the City of Angels, and Rome, the Eternal City, are cities saturated in prayer, reverence, and hedonism—frequently all at once, and often side by side. Their dual realities depend not on facts, but on faith—and they have long been magnets for pilgrims, tourists, scholars, shoppers, the genuinely curious, and the positively doomed.

There is much to see, and even more to experience. Some say too much—as these testaments to what is best and worst, are inundated with buildings designed for both devotion and dreams. They are cities of intensity; at times seething with confidence, at intervals plunged into despair. One tourist who has been to both said, "What I see tires me, and I what I don't see worries me."

Like Bangkok, Rome is a city that chokes on its own exhalations, thereby giving us *two* shrieking habitations that drown their own inhabitants in noise—and they endure it like addicts in denial. It is little wonder their respective leaders consistently make bad decisions. They can't hear a damn thing anyone is saying.

They are also unified by a succession of prime ministers who just cannot forgive the truth. Since 1945, Italy has had 56 governments, and Thailand 24 prime ministers. One could almost be tempted to think it was a competition.

When Julius Caesar said after the Battle of Zela, "Veni, vidi, vici"—I came, I saw, I conquered—it ranked as the most famous military message for 1,900 years. That is until the Thais arrived in force in Rome in the early eighties and announced, "We came, we saw, we bought the lot."

Rome was once cruel, and is now romantic. Bangkok was once romantic, and is now heartbroken. From being the Venice of the East, it's become the Toyota of the Moment. While most of ancient Rome lies on its side among the fallen columns of history, old Bangkok is now endangered and surrounded by the abandoned masonry of bankruptcy.

Both cities have become monuments to their own passing, and yet both the Romans and the Thais share a deep love of family, food, good company, and past glories. Their respective elites reflect a mutual vanity, a similar arrogance, and, sometimes, the most appalling taste. But it has to be said that the Christian city of Rome blew a real cuisine marketing opportunity with The Last Supper. It was the most famous meal in history, and yet no one has a fucking clue what was on the menu.

Perhaps to compensate, both elites dine to be seen, and eat to the soundtrack of privileged gossip—which they then spread with their mobile phones, often just to interrupt the food.

Similarly, these cities of history have neglected quarters littered with buildings with a frightening tendency to crumble—but, in defiance of time, somehow remain upright. For a while, I lived in the Trastevere district of Rome, in a dwindling garrison of aged nuns who let rooms out to phoney bohemians and real bums. It had one creaking elevator and it didn't matter which button you pressed, you always ended up in the kitchen. Once outside, you were accosted by the vapours of drunks who lay motionless in the medieval alleys.

In a stinking subway, someone had scrawled, "PRAY FOR ME" on the wall—to which someone else had added, "SURE."

It is not so different in parts of Bangkok. When I first arrived, I had one address. I was directed from the park to turn left into the "dismal rat hole at the side of the abandoned cinema," left again along "the open drain—you can't miss it," then to follow "the three most depressing alleys running east until you feel like killing yourself." I would eventually find myself in front of "something that looks like a hotel after Megadeth played a gig there—you'll know it by the gloom." This soon revealed itself as flattery. And it became my home. Which is another story somewhere else.

Still on this earthy level, Rome brims with homeless cats, while Bangkok bulges with unemployed dogs—both of whom would vomit with envy if they knew just how good life is for a rat in the Vatican.

The Eternal City is the bastion of Catholics who believe in the soul and everlasting life. You could spend an eternity in Rome just tombspotting. Bangkok is the divine fulcrum of Buddhism, whose followers believe in the self and the likelihood of more lifetimes to come—just to get it right.

Living here, I have come to suspect that if eternity does exist, it would resemble the Mah Boon Krong shopping centre on a Sunday afternoon; seething with humanity, hustling for a bargain, and all done with a smile.

Finally, take the traffic. Please. Roman traffic is famous for both its theatre and noise. To the Italians, a gridlock is an invitation to get involved. One minute they're shaking their fists and shouting abuse at any car within earshot, the next minute they're discussing it—deeply, *passionately*—and quite possibly planning the next one. It's opera. It's Latin. And it's a tragedy.

As a result, the Italian commuter arrives home a total wreck, looking as though he has been, well, crucified.

In Bangkok, the Thais simply sit and wait, resigned and relaxed with their fate. The horns are silent. The road rage is contained. It is peace in action. As a result, the Bangkok commuter arrives home late, but composed. Yet, I have long wondered what the Thais do with their frustration.

Now I think I know.

They spend it.

Stiff Upper Brits

The British Club in Bangkok smells like my old school. I am not a member of the club, and I was expelled from school—which perhaps makes the faint but familiar whiff of carbolic and polish that pervades the wooden floors and elegant staircase all the more poignant and terrifying.

On the few occasions I've been there, I'm petrified that a booming voice in the Churchill Bar will suddenly announce, "Will the boy who wrote the disgusting word on the blackboard in Form 4B this morning come to my study after lunch. That means you Beaumont."

It is a fine and handsome building, comfortably nestled in a colonial enclave surrounded by tended lawns and tennis courts. Although the building is painted brilliant white, and seems to stand smartly to attention—in step and in tune with the corporate nineties—to me, it is history dipped in sepia. An outpost of an ideal; a school away from home, a home away from school.

I enjoy going there, when I'm invited, but feel strangely elated when I leave—as though it's the last day of term. If I still had a school cap, I'd throw it in the air.

But the club hasn't always been just a residence of standards and stability for those far from home. It has also acted as an important fulcrum for serious decisions taken in times of real need. During the research of a book I've been writing—which has been going on for so long, I keep bumping into characters from earlier chapters who are complete strangers—I came across the unpublished diary of an English trader who was working in the city just before this country was occupied by the Japanese army in the last days of 1941.

"On Saturday evening, Dec 6th, a dance and fete were held at the British Club. It was a combination of many of the seasonal activities: the annual Winter Dance, a postponed St. Andrew's Day, a fete to raise money for the "Spitfire Fund" and so on, and 'all Bangkok' was there. About midnight the British and American ministers were recalled to their respective Legations to receive signals from Whitehall and Washington. We now know that these were warnings that a Japanese Task Force had been sighted off the coast of Indo-China heading in the direction of Thailand and the Malayan peninsula. Had the British Ambassador, Sir Josiah Crosby, summoned a meeting on that Sunday morning and imparted this news, more might well have escaped before the Japanese landed. Rumours were rife, but many of us were hardly in the right state of mind to give them serious thought after a long night of revelry."

Time would not even allow the dignity of a decent hangover. The following evening, Sir Josiah Crosby addressed a meeting of the British community at the club:

"He told us that he'd been assured by the Thai Foreign Office that all British subjects would be free to move about and continue their normal business; for those who could be spared and wanted to leave, he had been promised a special evacuation train. In the meantime he considered it was our duty to carry on as usual. The gathering was very sceptical and started to ask awkward questions at which Crosby lost his temper and stalked off the stage to growls of strong disapproval . . ."

With the benefit of hindsight, Sir Josiah Crosby seems to have been a complete prat. The "evacuation train" was a myth—as our trader soon discovered when he reached Hualamphong Station:

"A seething mass, managed to buy four platform tickets . . . every carriage was packed with people clambering through the windows. We squatted in the aisle on our suitcases overlaid by scores of children. It was devilish hot. We had no food but a tin of biscuits and a bottle of whiskey. All had a tot after we left to keep the "cold" out. All went well at first, but nemesis overtook us at the railhead at Lopburi. On the platform were detachments of Japanese soldiers and we were ordered out of the train. We stood there in the full sunshine, the centre of hundreds of eyes, for most of Lopburi had gathered to watch the fun."

Our trader was arrested, along with 15 other British civilians, and taken back under armed guard to Bangkok by bus. The Japanese commanding officer in Lopburi said, "You have nothing to fear from any Japanese officer or soldier and wished us good luck."

On New Year's Day, 1942, they were taken to an internment camp behind Thammasat University, where they joined 201 British internees—149 males and 52 females including children—along with members of the American and Dutch communities. Sir Samuel Brighouse, the chairman of the British Club, was also arrested, and, despite being allowed by the Japanese to receive special treatment in Saigon later in the war, he died of cancer on the 18th May, 1944.

Most remained in the camp until September 1945, when the 7th British Indian division arrived in Bangkok. Some died of illness, some were nearly killed by Allied bombers using the Chao Phraya as a navigation marker, and everyone complained about the food, the floods, and each other. Despite these difficulties, they should have been thankful that they were *where* they were.

It may have been a bad dream, but the barbed wire protected them from the real nightmare beginning to take place in the daylight, just a few hours west of the capital— along the Thai-Burma railway.

New Age
Gunpowder Plot

As it's November, perhaps the talk should be of revolt. Why? Because I went to the same school—St. Peter's, York— as Guy Fawkes. He and his gang were unfortunately sprung as they fiddled with fuses, gunpowder, and damp wicks underneath the Houses of Parliament in London on a perfectly fogged evening nearly four centuries ago.

The plot was fine, it was the matches and the script that were so inept.

I was sprung as I was jumping over the boarding school wall at midnight, and was sent home forever. The bastards even took away my lighter. *Just* in case.

We share not only an educational bond of failure, but also the occasional desire to blow things apart—even if it's only someone's ego or lifestyle. For me, a prime target would be the New Agers. I have a built-in skepticism about this movement, partly because I was a New Age person before the term was even invented—and long ago became a 'Real Age' person without even knowing it.

The frustration of talking to alien abductees and immortal beings was that the conversation was usually off the planet.

And why do all these self-appointed gurus of rebirthing all claim that they and their clients were romantic figures in their past? They were either Cleopatra's handmaiden, or a Japanese samurai, or Chief White Eagle. Why wasn't anyone a bus conductor in Dhaka, or a toilet cleaner in Omsk?

The other hassle I have with New Age disciples is that although they proclaim tolerance and compassion, few have been in a situation where either has been tested.

It's all very well to sit cross-legged behind closed eyes in a cloistered *ashram* halfway up the Himalayas. I know because I've done it. They should try coming out from under their spiritual umbrellas and hit Calcutta during the monsoon—surrounded by the dead, the desperate, and the stench—and see how they do. If they say this isn't reality, then they should keep taking the tofu. Reality or not, it happens. I know because I've seen it.

I met two "crusties" last week in Bangkok. A crustie is a New Age traveller who does the rock festival and save the whale circuit. Some live in caravans, others live in hedges; all of them live on welfare. They took over from where the hippies left off, which was a big mistake, because we hippies weren't going anywhere anyway. Like grunge music, crusties are a weird blend of apathy and aggression.

They wear Doc Martin boots, which are such a hassle to lace up, that once they get them on, they never take them off.

"Yep, 1989," said one, proudly patting his pair as if it was the day he graduated.

He was called "Mike Who Works," and was travelling with a friend called "Radiator" who obviously didn't. They had been up in Chiang Saen, and my intuition told me it wasn't for the view.

"I'm a professional beggar," said Radiator—who had a definite odour, but it wasn't of sanity.

"Can't you find work in the UK?"

He looked at me as though I was the alien—while they looked like part of a tramp convention.

"Nah. Can't leave me dog tied up to a hedge all day, can I?"

"So how did you get the money to come to Thailand?" I asked. They both shifted uncomfortably.

"While I begged, Mike lifted the wallets."

"It's the dog that created the diversion," insisted Mike, as though it was the dog's fault.

"Oh, is he friendly?"

"No, just incredibly smelly."

Like all the cars I have owned, these two guys were in various stages of illegality, immobility, and disintegration. Permanently damaged by the dole and heavy metal, they intended to beg here so as to get back to England to beg *there*.

Makes you wonder that the interesting thing about Stonehenge is not how it was built, but how it was financed.

"Got any money?" they said, almost in unison.

"No," I said honestly, looking nervously around for a dog.

"Got a light then?"

"Ah, I may be able to help you there . . ."

The boots alone would have blown the *soi* up. Just like bonfire night. And I was *burning* with the temptation.

Psst! Bubonic Plague! Pass it On!

I'm being constantly hassled by my determined, yellow-eyed girlfriend to write something about the environment here. My first reaction was, "What environment? And will you please remove your tail from the sofa, it's leaving scales all over the place."

I tried. I angled for truth and wrote, "Less than two hundred years ago ninety per cent of modern Thailand was covered in swamp and jungle, and was the province of the elephant and crocodile. There are now empty tracts where there were once forests, and there are now new forests which have been planted with seedlings that should never have been allowed into this country in the first place: namely the eucalyptus, which is neither indigenous, user-friendly, or farmer-welcome in Thailand's environment . . ."

My girlfriend coiled up closer and hissed, "No, the environment here in Bangkok. What can we save?"

"The dragon . . . ?" I ventured.

If I really knew the answer, I'd probably start my own religion. I'd even like to say something positive, but I've been in Bangkok long enough to know worse. My *soi* looks like Sarajevo—mortared, cratered, bombed out. The holes are full of water and filled with unknown creatures that blink and burp. It's as though nature herself has become a third-world country.

Only the rats look happy. They clean their whiskers and whisper sweet gossip to each other: "Psst! Bubonic plague, pass it on! Isn't it great?"

When it comes to saving, preserving, or conserving things in Bangkok, it's difficult to choose just one deserving candidate. The whole place is endangered. Sanity maybe? We may even be too late for that.

In Australia they save everything that has been named, stranded, or beached—and any building that has been standing long enough to form a cobweb is viewed as precious architectural heritage. The conservation movement is well funded, well organised, and unbalanced. Some of its members are so politically correct, they would marry the first whale they met. If that's not possible, they'll move in with a tree and hug it. Some trees have been hugged so much that they'll be suing for sexual harassment before long.

In England the cry was once, "Save the Morris Minor!" A noble car—but slower than a bicycle—which, when driven, is like being trapped inside a fifties radio. In East Berlin it was once, unfortunately, "Save the Trabant!" Which they couldn't because no one wanted it. Ironically, what few of them remain are now collectors items—but only for people in the free-wheeling West who never had to drive them in the wheel-clamped East.

Things can also become politically correct to the point of boredom. I live in the real world rather than the natural one—for better or for worse. I used to be an organic gardener. I have planted thousands of things, including weeds that were so attractive I encouraged them to grow in order to help me expand. But I do know one thing. Nature is not cute. It is neither fluffy nor cuddly. It is not a voice-over by

David Attenborough with music by Stravinsky. The Serengeti plain in Africa at sundown is a veritable abattoir. It's messy, bloody, and it's called the evening meal. And gatecrashers abound.

This planet has lost species of animals and plants the vast majority of us never even got to meet, let alone eat. Wolves and bears and eagles get saved because they're sexy. An endangered worm at the bottom of the ocean, glowing or not, is not sexy. Result? Extinction.

And by the way, why is it always *man* who is nature's greatest enemy? What were the women doing when we were hunting and gathering? Making tofu? Note to the politically correct: Must try harder.

So what *can* be saved here? Will we rally to the cry of, "Save the BMW!" or "Save Your Breath?" Or will the good citizens of this vast and vibrant metropolis find a real balance and shout, "Save US!"

From who? From ourselves and rampaging critters. Pity the tea picker who works on the edge of a tiger reserve in a national park. Is he nervous or what? Bangkok can only save its inhabitants from what it has created itself—which is the barbed wire air we have to breathe, and the unhealthiness of it all. Money has replaced balance. Greed has replaced integrity. And it will have to paid for. The meek may inherit the earth, but will they want it?

What this city needs is not more investment but more consciousness. Bangkok's problems have been created by humans and they're going to have to be solved by them.

Mahatma Gandhi was once asked by a rookie journalist what he thought of civilisation on this planet. The great man briefly stopped his spinning wheel and replied, "I think it would be a good idea." Indeed.

Christmas Past

I come from a land where the wind is permanently busy. Summer holidays were often spent dying of exposure behind a sand dune while eating boiled eggs, or—on the few days of sun—lying gormless among the li-los thirty yards out to sea, and slowly drifting towards France.

In deep December we went to school in the dark and we came home in the dark—and all I remember is the elements going sideways at fifty miles an hour and *leaning* into them to stay upright. The forecast on the radio was the same every day for five months: "Sunny periods with sleet spreading from the east," or "Sun glimpsed in Scotland. Police baffled . . ." Breakfast was hot porridge and golden syrup, and by November our dreams were only of Christmas.

We were polite kids, northern, and spirited. We were always cheeky and over-excited. Trouble was not a stranger. Every Christmas Eve, we went carol singing. We never rang the bell at a house. We'd just stand, wrapped from head to foot in scarves and balaclavas, and sing our thing. The carols always sounded muffled, as though they were being sung from underneath a blanket—which, in a sense, they were.

After three verses of "Silent Night," our teeth would be chattering so much that we sounded like Muppets with frostbite—and then suddenly we'd all be *hammering* on the door for money, warmth, *anything* to get us out of that Arctic blast. By the time someone finally opened the door, we'd all be crying. It was pathetic.

One year, we played a soccer match in a snowstorm on the last day of term. It was like midnight at the South Pole. You couldn't see your own feet, and we never found the goal. We never even found the *ball*. There was only the sound of ghostly voices, lost and searching . . . "Over here!" "Where?" "*Here*!" and "I want my mum . . ." The referee's whistle blew from somewhere far away and then silence. It was eerie. Shapes would loom out of the storm and then disappear like drunken *yetis*. Occasionally they crashed into each other. The ground was frozen solid and there was a dull thud followed by a low moan whenever bodies landed on it. It was ludicrous. And it was real.

On Christmas Eve 1972, I was in the cellar of a hotel in Kabul, Afghanistan, when a bomb landed in the garden. The door crashed open and the fat Afghan hotel manager was yelling, "Goo d'etat! Goo d'etat! You must be leaving!!" Through an organic fog of herbal fragrance, an American drawled, "We ain't goin' *nowhere* man."

How true. On Christmas morning we emerged and stood around admiring the massive crater on the lawn. There hadn't, in fact, been a "Goo d'etat." The carnage had been the work of one very unhappy and extremely drunk Afghan pilot. Having found the airport, he had then found the only jet that worked, and roared off to bomb the palace. He had missed his target by a quarter of a mile. The American said it was outstanding.

At dawn on Christmas morning 1982, I walked along the edge of the Pacific Ocean in Northeast Australia on an endless, deserted beach. The sea was all power and show that morning—vast, crystal blue, clean as a tear. I had the universe to myself and applauded the director.

That afternoon I drove inland to an invitation: Christmas lunch on an outback commune. It was 47 degrees. I drove through a small town called WHY, and then further up the road, another hamlet called WHY NOT. There was a sign outside the only garage:

"CHRISTMAS CHOOK. HALF-DEAD. $1.50."

So I bought it.

At the commune, it was given to the working dogs as a present. Later on, a hippy came up with a bit of feather dangling off his lip and told me it was delicious.

On Christmas night in 1987, I was at some outdoor rave in Freemantle, Western Australia. The whole crowd was three sheets to the wind and swayed in all directions—to the music, to the drink, and for the hell of it. Wobbling off home on my bicycle felt like riding on two rubber bands. When the motorbike crashed into me, everything was airborne—but on landing we were both too drunk to be badly hurt. The biker thought it was hilarious and kept laughing. So I sat on him. And waited for the police.

When they arrived, they arrested me for trying to squash him. I couldn't argue with that. At the police station an hour later, the duty sergeant pressed ten bucks into my hand and said, "Take this and drink it. Walk home and Happy Christmas."

"Why zank you osshifer . . . an' Happy Christmas to you too."

IS THIS WHAT YOU WANT ROGER?

THE ILLUSTRATIONS OF

HANN WIN

And then there was Celine . . .

We used to *eat* Englishmen . . .

"Well, that's it. I'm off . . ."

His journey continued to fascinate me . . .

. . . vacation in the land of virtual reality . . .

I asked to see the Dalai Lama. "He's in Dublin . . ."

"*Greet* mon!" he said, crunching away . . .

. . . turn left if you want to reach Mae Hong Son,
1,739 curves away . . .

. . . with laughter coming through the open windows . . .

The class clapped as I started to strum the barbed wire . . .

Our picture opens on a turquoise sea . . .

I now live between a slum and a disaster . . .

. . . this city is forever changing your plans . . .

Is he nervous or what?

"I think it would be a good idea . . ."

"*Nyet*! I found one," he snapped . . .

Trouble was not a stranger . . .

. . . I knew from the tone of her voice
that somebody was doomed . . .

"... SWIM YOU PRAT ..."

... can't even organise a bucket in a monsoon ...

"I'm terribly sorry, I didn't know it was *necessary* anymore . . ."

. . . behind the saffron and the smile . . .

The Business of Pleasure

The spirit house outside the Imperial Queen's Park Hotel is slightly bigger than my first apartment. Believe me, these spirits have got it made. With a nice view overlooking the park, it wouldn't surprise me if, under that little wooden roof, there was an *ensuite* bathroom, tiny "Emporium" scatter cushions, and cable TV.

From the park, there is a discreet path that leads to the back of the hotel, which passes this spiritual condo, and then up the stairs into a restaurant, in which I have eaten once or twice. It's a nice restaurant with polite food. I remember the roast lamb being impeccable; it was a lamb you could have taken anywhere.

There is also a small sign by the glass door which reads, "Hotel guests are welcome to use the gate into the park, which closes at 8 p.m." It's all so civilised—and a far cry from the scruffy, beer-stained sign nailed on to the back door of my student lodgings in London which read, "Please don't vomit on the floor, what do you think the seats are for?"

I have to confess that I use this impressive hotel as a short cut to my humble abode a few metres from the main entrance. After walking through the slum that is Klong Toey, it's comforting—once I've got rid of the guilt—to feel the cool opulence of the marble floors, and to breathe the scent of expense, after the stench of poverty.

One of the house butlers, Keith Dellar, has noticed my regular deviations, because, as a butler, he sees everything. He also knows that I know that he knows it. It's all part of his job.

We've been on friendly terms for some years now, and I often call out, "Good evening squire," to him across the hotel lobby, which, these days, seems crammed with Japanese tourists. He may often reply with, "Good evening my lord, we're a dying breed," over their heads. Being dressed in jeans and a T-shirt, it's always a buzz to be referred to in that language, and even more of a buzz to see the Japanese looking totally bewildered at the interchange.

Keith Dellar and Julio Duque are full-time resident butlers, positions they have held since 1992, when they were asked by Akorn Hoontrakul—the then head of the Imperial Group, whom they had met in London that year—to come to Thailand. It was a shrewd move, and stamped with the class it delivered.

I had many questions for Keith, questions I'd always wanted to ask a butler, but had never had the chance because, somehow, I'd never actually got around to having a butler of my own.

Resplendent in their formal morning dress, with a fresh rose in their respective buttonholes, roaming the restaurants and hovering in the grand lobby, do they sometimes get mistaken for being the manager?

"Oh yes, often," says Keith. "We've also been mistaken for wedding guests and classical conductors. Some guests even ask me if I'm the owner."

"Does that bother you?"

"Not a bit. But it might bother him," he said grinning.

As professional butlers for over forty years, both Dellar and Duque treat everyone as an equal, whether they be of the landed gentry or those who have just landed gently, a titled gentleman, or the third wife of a Toyota dealer from Cambodia. It makes no difference. Why?

Because they are paying.

Ah. So the customer, even if he's an arrogant prat who can't even spell the word "manners" and doesn't have a clue what's going on around him, is always right. Right?

"Absolutely, yes," says Keith with complete conviction.

I would have a big problem with that. In fact I *do* have a big problem with that—and it's one of the reasons why I've never worked in the service industry.

I simply don't have the right disposition. I would rather dig ditches than serve table. And I have. I find it impossible to serve people who are ruder and more arrogant than either the people I work for, or with.

And to be honest, I'm not such a good guest either. Whenever I get the rare chance to stay in a quality hotel, I don't so much occupy a room as disturb it. I immediately turn everything on, and then steal everything in the bathroom—including the sewing kit and those cotton wool thingies. After all, there's no crime like the present, and what's more, one is actually paying for the privilege to pilfer. I always look twice at the sumptuous bath robes, but I know I'll get sprung. And when I'm guilty, I blush. Even when there's no one around.

However, there's always one rule, shared by millions. *Never* touch the mini bar. I have worked out that if you drank and ate everything in the mini bar of a downtown Tokyo hotel, it would equal the gross national output of a small African country—and that's in a good year.

"We do have our ways at getting back at the truly rude," Keith conceded, looking inscrutable. I raised an eyebrow in conspiratorial hope. But nothing doing. No trade secrets.

But this is to miss the point. Taking care of people, rather than merely serving them, are two very different things. "The essence of being a butler is to make sure everything is in order, from beginning to end," Keith explains.

A butler doesn't serve at a table, but will notice from a thousand paces that a foreign minister's champagne glass may need refilling—and with the slightest nod to a waiter, it's done.

Neither is a butler a manager. Despite his knowledge of wines, cutlery, cuisine, and etiquette—the very arts of service—he is, in essence, a professional socialiser who's role is both intimate and courteous.

And these two men should know, for they have worked at the very highest echelons of British society, in the fine houses and grand estates belonging to the Duke of Marlborough, the Duke of Westminster, the Duke of Norfolk, and many more. Keith maintains that the British aristocracy are still the best people to work for: "They are down to earth and real, unlike the *nouveau riche*, who may own beautiful homes, but it's all terribly artificial. One is there simply for show."

Indeed. For discretion, one of the hallmarks of a true butler, can't apply if the employer is incapable of being discrete.

They have also been in the employ of the British royal family, especially Princess Diana and the Queen Mother—who is famous for her fondness for dry Martinis, public service, and wicked sense of humour.

Years ago, Keith told me, she would host regular parties at Clarence House in London. On one occasion, the Queen's dress designers had been invited, including Hardy Amies, Norman Hartwell, and the like—gentleman all, and all tactfully described as "light on their feet." At one point, the Queen Mother went upstairs, leaving the men drinking and chatting away. For some reason she couldn't come down at once, and said loudly, "When you queens have finished down there, there's an old queen who wants a gin and tonic up here."

So, what are the best parts of the job? Or was that one of them?

"When I worked in the grander households, the best part was that you always saw people at their best," says Keith. "They were either entertaining, or being entertained."

And if they are saddened by anything, it is the slow decline in standards over the years—from manners to dress code. A levelling out. A dilution of excellence.

However, butlers are not are dying breed; it's the world for which they were originally trained that is the endangered species. As hospitality schools now turn out "professionals" after a mere two years, they are feeding a society that places show over depth, style over form, and noise over music.

Yet true butlers still retain their own code, and their own humour. They can turn things around if it suits them. Take the story of Lady Cunard, of the fabulous luxury liner fortune. One evening, she held a large and important dinner party at which her long-serving and badly-paid butler became very drunk.

Anxious and indignant, she scribbled something on a piece of paper and handed it to him. It said, "You are drunk. Please go to bed *at once*." The butler took the note, nodded, swayed a bit, and walked around the table and handed the message to the British prime minister.

They say you should judge a hotel by the quality of its guests. I disagree. I believe it should be judged by the class of its staff.

A Class Apart

The English are renowned for failing to learn other languages, preferring to shout even louder at uncomprehending foreigners. So why any of them would want to *teach* English as a foreign language is something of a mystery.

Is it a hereditary thing? An intuitive calling to a righteous and noble career? To do good, to nourish other minds?

Or is it just a convenient way of being paid to see the planet before settling down to, well, more *important* things.

Whatever the motivation, English teachers form a sizeable community of expats here—although they are quite separate from Bangkok's legions of company men and their families. But they remain the target of cynics, who, at dinner parties, delight in trotting out that exhausted cliché, "Those who can, do. Those who can't, teach."

Funnily enough, many cynics are incapable of either. For that's what a cynic does best: nothing.

But wait. This is Bangkok now, and for many teachers I know, the job is less of a calling and more of a means of survival. It *might* only turn into a calling after they've struggled through the toxic assault and crossed town in a sprightly four days, only to be paid the princely sum of 250 baht an hour.

But there is also a class structure within the teaching community in Bangkok, and I am not so much concerned here with the career teacher employed by international schools or meaningful universities—both of which recruit the vast majority of their teachers overseas, and who require more qualifications and special expertise than a fighter pilot. No, I'm interested in the "underground"—that circuit of teaching that doesn't officially exist in this city, but actually numbers something around 3,000 people—most of them men. Whatever its legal status, freelance, private teaching is a thriving, vital service that has nothing to do with school ties, bells, and assembly at 7 a.m. I know this because I was one.

Freelance teachers are an interesting species. Indeed, David Attenborough's upcoming nature series, *Teacher Spotting on the Great Sukhumvit Massif*, is a fascinating study of this peculiar tribe:

"It was in places like this, millions of years ago, that TEFLman was first seen. Shy, nocturnal creatures, they like to drink copiously and dribble a lot. They tend to be tall, thin, pallid, and sweaty, and they carry briefcases and have a glazed look which suggests they're lost in space but deep in therapy. They move uncertainly through the Bangkok throng, and can be seen planning lessons and muttering to themselves at bus stops, 'I have a cat, you have a cat . . . '"

So, for those of you who have just arrived in Bangkok and your TEFL certificate is beginning to smudge under your over-heated armpit as you do the rounds of the language schools in Siam Square, let me offer a few tips, observations, and lies to remember.

LESSON 1: WHY BE A TEACHER IN BANGKOK IN THE FIRST PLACE FOR GOD'S SAKE?

Money? Doubtful.

Altruism? Possibly.

Sex? Quite likely.

The reasons are myriad, the outcome uncertain. Qualified or not, most teachers arrive here thinking a semi-colon is an intestinal problem—and nearly all leave believing it is. That's usually all they have left.

Some people are passing through and use teaching as a means to dip into the culture and move on. But the vast majority of teachers who plan to stay a while have to be wrung through the language school system to learn the ropes, pay the rent, and gain valuable experience at the coalface. As their contacts expand and their confidence grows, their livers start to buckle. Then they nick a couple of students from the company and *voila*—they're in business.

And the true beauty about being a private teacher is that one is not bound by any curriculum. It's loose, free, and comes under the vague heading of English Conversation. And think about it; what other job could possibly take you into the very heart of Thai society—from the rich to the poor, from the hotels and big boy companies, to the private home and the slum?

Answer? None.

Come. Let's be honest. This is life, this is not a rehearsal. We want to thrive not survive. Which brings us to the subject of . . .

LESSON 2: THE "BAHTABILITY FACTOR"

It varies, but if, after a year, you're still making less than 250 baht an hour, it's time for a serious reality check. This is rice money, and I sincerely hope you're not teaching "Business" English. If *you* aren't making it, how the hell do you expect your students to?

There are private teachers out there making up to 1,000 baht an hour. I know some teachers who won't get out of *bed* for less than 500 baht. Actually, I know some teachers who won't get out of bed at all.

Greedy? Arrogant? I don't think so. In this mad metropolis the first rule of survival for the private teacher—indeed for everyone—is to work smart, not hard.

So, depending on qualifications, persistence, lying, and serious grovelling, one's monthly income can oscillate anywhere between 20,000 and 50,000 baht a month. If you're making less than the former, *get out of bed this minute!* And if you're making the latter, give me a call *right now!*

LESSON 3: THE OFFICIAL ALTERNATIVE

During a job interview at a language school, when they've just offered you 150 baht an hour for three months while "on probation" (a cheap trick which can make you feel guilty having spent 2,500 dollars on a TEFL course that actually *qualifies* you to be a teacher), feel perfectly free to ask the interviewer what *his* qualifications are.

Then look and see if the carpets are nailed to the floor.

Oh, and don't forget to ask him what the school is charging the student. If he tells you, he's probably lying. If he refuses, then you know he is.

With these experiences you will quickly discover that language schools are neither altruistic nor charitable institutions. They are a business. Know your worth; it can get messy out there.

LESSON 4: GET TO KNOW YOUR STUDENTS

Evaluation is very important. To get the most out of a company's staff, it's important that the students are at the same level of understanding, ignorance, or both. To achieve this, a brief interview with each student will be very helpful in deciding which class level they should attend.

"What's your name?"

"I'm fine thank you."

"OK, fine. Where are you from?"

"I'm 17, nek month"

Yes. Right. Elementary, I think. Next?

I asked one stunningly beautiful Thai girl at a certain company that sells books if she spoke any English. She smiled and replied in the affirmative. My knees buckled. I asked her to give me an example of her command of the language. She only knew one sentence, but said it perfectly:

"The man over there will pay."

LESSON 5: TEACHER TYPES AND TRAITS

You can always tell the health of a teacher by looking at his mouth. If it's shut he's dead. You can also spot them from two hundred metres away, and it's usually the diet that gives them away: rice, Singha beer, and Swan's *Practical English Usage*.

Type 1: They look awful. They're always ill. They never smile, and they take themselves *very* seriously. They are on a mission. They actually *study* the curriculum, and I've heard that some even sleep with it. But like do-gooders who hit the go-go bars and recoil in horror, they always fail to notice the obvious; the students and the whores aren't the problem—and *they* certainly aren't the solution. These teachers are *academic*. You meet them in bars and on buses. They talk to you with enthusiasm, you nod in agreement, and then nod off with boredom. If they have this effect on their own contemporaries, imagine the effect they have on their students.

Type 2: They hail from North Yorkshire and Southern Alabama. They come equipped with an extremity of accents that even their own mothers would have difficulty deciphering. Both sound as if they have just drunk either 15 pints of untreated Scrumpy, or a quart of bourbon and half a

Viagra. And they wonder why 30 of their students have fallen asleep and 17 never turned up at all.

Type 3: The Renaissance teacher. If language teaching is about anything, it's about communication. It's both the medium and the message. The Renaissance teacher knows this instinctively. He may be pony-tailed, slightly eccentric, and have a library of past lives you wouldn't want to show your mother, but nonetheless, he's interesting and interested. He entertains as he teaches, and his teaching is entertaining.

He is aware that Thais are a fun-loving people, and that when he arrives for class, his students have already worked an eight hour day and don't want a bland teacher doing dumb things on a whiteboard. So he throws the *Cambridge Book of Mindnumbing Exercises* over his shoulder and says with a grin, "Let's learn this thing *together*."

The Renaissance teacher has both the props and the direction, but it's his spontaneity that ignites the magic and inspires the student. Money is usually the furthest thing from his mind—and, more often, his wallet. Most of these independent characters are funny, self-effacing, and love what they are doing. They are wired differently. And thank God for that; this city needs them.

LESSON 6: CANCELLATION EXCUSES

In any culture cancellations are a hassle. In Thailand they are a riot. For the private teacher they are an alien virus that can strike at any time. The diary may look healthy at the beginning of the month. Sums are done on the back of beermats and envelopes. Things look peachy. You may even be able to make the rent. And then the phone rings.

"Me no come." Click.

"The buffalo died." Click.

"Solly teacher. No have time." Click.

"I have cancer of the colon. But come tomollow." Click.

Teachers need their escape routes too.

"Nn . . ." Click.

"Forgot. Dentist." Click.

"Can't find you." Click. (Never tried).

"In Penang." Click.

LESSON 7: NIGHTMARE 1—THE KNOCK ON THE DOOR

"What was that again officer? Brian Smith did you say? His work permit? Ah, yes, terribly sorry. Accident you know. Didn't see a thing, but I heard it was *awful*. He flew to Zimbabwe for brain surgery. No, he wasn't flying the plane himself. Gosh! Is that the time?"

LESSON 8: NIGHTMARE 2—CAUGHT ON THE JOB

Being seen at 5.30 a.m. outside the Thermae squashed in a *tuk-tuk* with four girls who are giggling in your ear. An expensive car pulls up alongside. A rear window winds down. It's one of your female students. She is accompanying her parents to the local *wat*.

"Hello Teacher," your pupil says brightly.

The parents say nothing. They don't have to. Their expressions say it all; a facial cocktail of horror and disgust.

The girls wave. You cringe. And there's absolutely nowhere to hide. Busted.

Hours later you wake up from a sweat-drenched nightmare. You go to the bathroom and look into the mirror, and your worst fears are confirmed. There is no reflection. You have lost face. All of it.

LESSON 9: THE BENEFITS OF AN UNOFFICIAL PROFESSION

Let's put it this way. If you come to Thailand as backpacker, what do you really see? Who do you really meet?

You meet other backpackers. Often in brain-dead bars watching bad, loud, videos. You see temples and beaches and more backpackers. But do you touch the culture, and does it really get a chance to touch you?

Equally, if you're sent here as an architect, an engineer, an adman, or an administrator, the chances are you will be housed, driven, and catered for. You may socialise at swish hotels in refined settings and get to meet important, corporate people, but it's a sterile, hermetically-sealed existence. If your ambition is to truly immerse yourself into the very heartbeat of Bangkok, then nothing comes close to being a language teacher.

I have taught in private homes and public hospitals, huge companies and tiny offices. I've taught slum kids and hilltribe kids, and farmers sons and street vendors daughters. I have visited hundreds of Thai people in their own environment, to teach them this ridiculous language with its absurd rules and quirky meanings. I have glimpsed their realities, even though I will always be in the shadow of the meanings that forge them. I feel honoured and privileged to have taught these people, and immeasurably enriched by their warmth, shyness, and beauty.

And I've even been paid for it when I remembered to get out of bed.

Thongs for the Memory

Today's subject is manners. That's mainly because the "making *origami* elephants" idea fell through. A few of us have been pondering, over a glass or three, the importance of common civility—and, surprise and no surprise, I think I'm becoming exactly like my parents.

I *knew* it would happen one day—even after a long and thoroughly decadent apprenticeship of trying to avoid it. But despite delving into dope dens in distant lands, seeking sex, sandalwood, and salvation anywhere I could, and permanently living beyond my means, it has done nothing to avoid this destiny. Shit. I can't even get arrested anymore.

But in the midst of hedonism there is no perspective. Indeed, why should there be?

However, my moral conditioning did instill in me how to conduct myself in far-off and unknown cultures—as a representative of the whiter-shade-than-pale species. Be aware, sensitive, polite, and open. Apart from Hong Kong, where the crucial reality is money, and *only* money, I've found that in most Asian societies, manners are impeccable.

Unfortunately, all bad things come to an end, and as I dragged myself kicking and screaming away from certain vices and various harems of self-indulgence, I realised that it was time to be mugged by reality once again.

This has been compounded by a revelation. I was walking down Sukhumvit Road recently and noticed two foreign bratpackers arguing with breathtaking rudeness with a young, female, mute street-vendor.

The foreigners were both filthy, weighted, sweaty, and sartorially scant in Koh Samui beach grunge. One of them had a beard like a fully-grown nature reserve. He was an eco-system on legs. Winged things were entering and leaving it like drones from a mothership.

He wore a T-shirt which read, "VISIT NORTH KOREA BEFORE NORTH KOREA VISITS YOU," and wore boots the size of rice barges. His friend, who looked like Joe Cocker the morning after a bad gig—or a very good one—had hair that was receding faster then communism.

He was wearing one thong.

I'm a curious chap and asked, "Did you lose your thong?"

"*Nyet!* I found one," he snapped.

Wow, a Russian lucks out. Or did he? Discuss.

Did they care about their behaviour, their dress, their affect on others? Absolutely not. Taste didn't even get a chance to raise its head. Thais and foreigners alike were staring in justified horror, and wincing visibly at this feral performance.

It reminded me of a flight I took to Bali, on which three Australian Rules Football teams were also booked. Their idea of a holiday in someone else's country was a rebellion against common decency—and to hell with anybody who complained. They were already drunk when they got on the plane—and then they really got started. It was the only time I've ever seen someone vomit on the ceiling at 30,000 feet. An amazing and dreadful sight. It drips.

On arrival in Bali, they were still throwing up at passport control. The tiny-framed, exquisite Balinese just stared in stunned silence—and I just cringed in shame.

Well, excuse me while I adjust my halo, but I believe these types are a new breed—purpose built for insult, and dumbed down for convenience.

They are the 'Dead Character Society,' who thrive on the bliss of ignorance.

Maybe it's the ease and speed with which we can travel the global village that makes us insensitive to new cultures; cultures that may have the *facade* of concrete and fast food similar to our own, but are vastly different in character and substance—if we only took the time to discover it. In travel, assumption is always the mother of fuck-up.

As I turned away from the two on Sukhumvit, I couldn't help asking, "What time's your flight?"

They roared at me in synthetic fury and then shambled off—their knuckles dragging along the ground, elbowing the odd beggar, and spitting in front of bus stops.

They are the downwardly mobile. You could have walked across their brains without getting your feet wet.

Chivalry is by no means dead in this city, or indeed anywhere else—it's just suffering from a hernia, that's all.

Thanks. I feel much better now.

Are You Sitting Comfortably?

The kwanza may sound like the African version of the sexy Brazilian dance the *lambada*, but it is not. It is merely the currency of Angola—which is in such a bad way it can't even shake hands, let alone get up and jive.

I received a phone call from an old girlfriend who is working in the capital Luanda. I can't tell you what she does. Well I can, but I'd have to kill you afterwards. She told me you need 250,000 kwanzas to buy just one American dollar. Taking three mining executives out to dinner required two suitcases full of money. That was for the bill, not the bribe.

"It cost me 46 million kwanzas for three lousy prawn cocktails," she said down the crackling line. I dread to think what the phone call cost.

I love this kind of information; for this, to me, is the real news—first hand, off-the-cuff, pared down, warmed up.

It also goes to show that there are far more interesting realities in this world than CNN with it's flashflood of emotions. Just look at all the round-ups and wind-downs of the "important events" of 1996. Where were the following items? How come they slipped through the CNN net?

January 13th: Voodoo was adopted as the official religion of Benin.

January 18th: A British man who succeeded in becoming the first person ever to walk unaided to the South Pole rang home only to be told by his grandmother that he was completely stupid.

January 20th: A tenor fell off a ladder and died on stage at the Metropolitan Opera House in New York, immediately after singing the words, "Too bad you can only live so long."

February 27th: The first attempt by South African climbers to scale Mount Everest was in doubt after their leader threatened to kill the editor of a newspaper sponsoring his expedition.

March 2nd: Hundreds of thousands of yaks on the Changhai plateau in Western China froze to death in temperatures falling below minus 30 degrees centigrade.

April 11th: There were 22 million unemployed people across Europe.

May 13th: Applicants for motorcycle licenses in Indonesia were required to visit hospitals to see accident victims.

June 11th: Einstein's original theory of relativity was put up for auction at Sotheby's for 3.2 million pounds.

July 16th: This month, 82 years ago, the Battle of Passchendale opened in high summer in France. By October, the British had advanced some five miles and lost 275,000 men.

August 1st: Mr. Abdala Bucaram, a populist who campaigned under the name El Loco, was elected the president of Ecuador. He said he was the first madman to fill the post. Last week he was dismissed from office on the grounds of "mental incompetence."

August 3rd: The justice minister of Zimbabwe was disappointed by a lack of domestic applicants for the job of national hangman, although there was a flood of applications from Western Europe.

August 8th: Mr. Banhan Silpa-archa, the prime minister of Thailand, called upon young people in Bangkok to visit the zoo instead of nightclubs.

August 12th: Nuclear physicists searching for an obscure subatomic particle at the Cern Laboratory in Geneva found their efforts were being thwarted by two bottles of Heineken beer jammed into their accelerator.

August 28th: On this day, 60,000 people, 30,000 tons of freight, 10,000 cars, and 40 Eurostar trains passed through the Channel Tunnel. Two months later on November 18th, a freight train caught fire in the tunnel about 12 miles from France, causing considerable damage. Shares in Eurostar plummeted. (Shit, I own 20 of them).

September 17th: A total of 12,562 Taiwanese, including one aged 101, swam across a lake, apparently in an attempt to get themselves into the *Guinness Book of Records*.

September 18th: Seven pounds of heroin were found aboard a plane which had just flown President Samper of Columbia home from making an anti-drugs speech in New York.

September 21st: Doctors have estimated that a direct punch from Mike Tyson is the equivalent of having a 90 lb. weight dropped on your head from six feet when you're not looking.

October 10th: A wolf had killed its 12th victim in Uttar Pradesh in India.

October 10th: Saudi Arabia has beheaded 32 people so far this year. China had arrested 1.53 million prostitutes and their clients between 1991 and 1995.

October 17th: It was revealed that in early June, Sherpas had removed two tons of rubbish from Everest.

October 20th: At the Phuket Vegetarian Festival, devotees at a Chinese temple pierced various parts of their bodies with objects that included an anchor, a bath tap, and a 5 ft. marlin fish.

October 29th: A famous journalists bar in New York finally closed its door due to the high rent. The owner said, "It wasn't a bar for writers with a drinking problem, it was a bar for drinkers with a writing problem."

November 12th: A Zimbabwean MP was fined 66 pounds for biting off the upper lip of a fellow politician during talks to end the divisions in the ruling Zanu-PF Party. The lip was produced as evidence in court.

November 15th: A hotel in Sydney hoping to attract tourists for the 2000 Olympics, is offering the classic three course Australian breakfast—which consists of a cup of tea, a cigarette, and a look around.

December 2nd: According to the Institute for the Study of Drug Dependency in the UK, around a million ecstasy tablets were consumed in Britain each weekend in 1996. It has now grown into a 600-million-pound black market business.

Desperate Dispatches

Dear Mum,

Thanks for the belated birthday present, and yes, it bounced. So, here I am in Thailand. The weather is here, wish you were beautiful.

In your previous letter you described me as "a disturbed person." Well yes, but you have no idea how much. At the time, I was still working for grandmother as a piano player in a brothel in Macau, but I ran into a spot of bother.

I fell in love with a girl, who turned out to be a boy, who was distantly related to a liquorice baron—an Oriental spiv who only came out at night, and who inhabited the privileged world of entrenched villainy.

I managed to escape through the ugly crowd during the solo of "*Peelings, nothing more than peelings . . .*" and, passing myself off as an itinerant carpet-buyer, I lived a harumscarum existence in bazaars on both sides of the Afghan border until I was finally arrested in Singapore because my hair was one third of a millimetre too long. I was brave mum.

You would have been proud. I only allowed myself a small groan after the 59th lash.

Describe Bangkok you ask? It's a city of ordinary miracles; a place that, through the sheer calibre of its heritage, defies accountability. It's beguiling and shrewd. Its secrets do not bob on the surface, and like all cities of grace and wisdom, it takes time to discover her essence.

Forget the traffic, it ain't going anywhere—so the residents persist with life, pray for a solution, and improvise. But, as nobody can even *agree* on a plan, let alone implement one, I believe the city is actually a celestial test case. Somebody *knows* something, and one day we'll wake up and see, "HISTORY IS JUST A VAST EARLY WARNING SYSTEM," written in the smog above the city—so why fight it?

Yet people full of rush and expectation perceive Bangkok as merely a structural futility that generates chaos and frustrates the pursuit of wealth that built it in the first place. I like to consider it more as an environment of encouraging disarray. It's a riot of moneyed energy anyway, and, therefore, an honest reflection of human priorities. As a result, it is not cheap. In fact, money flies off you in all directions at once. High above the traffic, huge offices hum wealth, while down below the people jostle and whistle for opportunity.

Are you healthy? Funny you should ask. I only feel ill when I'm actually *outside* the city confines—and discover something called oxygen. I haven't seen a tree since 1991. I used to think my eyes were blue and piercing, but have recently been assured they are merely open and vacant. Perhaps this is due to a diet of vegan baps and vodka.

Is it safe? Well, yes and no. Lethal agricultural whiskey has led to many a local crime of passion, but then I'm not really surprised. The rural whiskey is like drinking Albanian anti-freeze. Personally, I have never felt so safe in my life, and I have staggered out of clubs I probably should never have gone into in the first place, at hours that were so late they were early. Awash in foolish vulnerability, I've giggled my way home.

Try that in South London and you'll wake up dead.

Why am I still here? Because of the challenge of the edge Mum, and . . . er . . . I'm neither a good carpet dealer nor a company man. I can't think corporate, so I have to think self-reliant, for this is a city that tests you—and that is a good character-building game. It's also the only game where you can smoke and drink on the pitch.

Am I learning anything? Well, if I wasn't, I'd be back in Ouagadougou playing Cat Stevens covers. The here and now is quite enough thank you, as Bangkok is an epic celebration that somehow manages to be relaxed in the furious energy of its own development.

Yet with the chance of success comes the risk of failure. But right now, Bangkok seems afraid of neither—although she has her critics.

Some of them continue to see the city as a university of sensual scholarship, and a place of such recent conceit that it could turn out to be spectacular in its failure. For others, it's a tuition in humility, and the opportunity to assist in the inevitable changes.

Survival? I did place an ad in the paper once: "Patron sought by ordinary genius. Please call." But my phone has been so quiet, it's practically audible.

Religion? I'm working on it. Compassion is in. I've even tacked some do's and don'ts on my door. Rule 3: "Unknown flying insects with wingspans that blot out the sun should only be killed in self defence."

By the way, the last glimpse I had of grandmother was of her lighting a cigar at tantalising length, whilst talking on the phone to the liquorice baron. I don't speak Cantonese, but I knew from her tone of voice that somebody was doomed.

Desperately
Seeking Sustenance

We wanted a restaurant where fine vintages were to be found. We wanted a restaurant where, when you asked what the *"Soup de jour"* was, the waiter did not disappear for ten minutes and come back with the reply, "It's the soup of the day sir."

It took me years to learn this: The price of something will always be vindicated by the person who is paying for it. I don't think it's necessarily a good lesson, but it is an important one.

So I suggested a place I'd heard of. We went in my friend's old jeep, which sounds as though it hasn't been serviced since the *Tet* offensive. He works for the UN. He's married but unhappy. In fact, he's been secretly in love with a Balinese girl for years, and when he finally met her, it had been so long, he had forgotten what it was he wanted to do to her.

"Where's the ashtray?" I asked.

"You're in it."

The back seat was liberally spread with the contents of a bachelor's fridge—including the bits of haggis my friend had nibbled on the Cambodian border on New Year's Eve.

The owner of the restaurant was called Enrico, and was quite well dressed for a thug. His sartorial demeanour displayed what few redeeming features he possessed. Like, he only had four mutilated, pierced body parts on public display. But he was certainly confused about how to greet people. Half of him wanted to be nice and welcoming, while the other half was suspicious and defensive—so his affectionate embrace was often accompanied by a knee to the groin. He was from Palermo.

He tried to be all things to all people, and ended up being nothing to any of them. Business was slow, and his accountant was changing colour by the day.

"Would you like a drink?" he asked.

"Yes, I think it's time to enter the spirit world."

"Oh, are you religious?"

"No. I just like vodka."

Enrico drove a Ferrari Testosteroné. He had the sperm count of a gerbil. He merely had to look at a female to make her pregnant. But where's the fun in that? He once seduced a society lady by blowing up the house they were staying in, rescuing her in her nightie, and wrapping himself around her for protection, and, ultimately, his pleasure. And I thought, you bastard. Why didn't I think of that?

The menu was an animal lover's nightmare.

"Would sir like the sheep's brains?"

"Uh, no thanks, I couldn't possibly eat something someone else has been thinking with."

"How about piglet's testicles?"

"Oh yes."

"How many?"

"Well, two please, naturally."

Halfway through the dead-snail salad, I was already prattling on about books when my friend said, "Shakespeare is so tiring. You never get a chance to sit down unless you're a king." So we talked money, women, and work. The usual fare. A safe itinerary.

Dessert was a large bowl of fruit. Such riches.

Clumsy and emotional after about 17 vodkas between us, we easily engaged the missionaries who were sitting at the next table. They were new to town. We asked them who they were trying to save, but they neatly side-stepped this trap and asked us about the rules of *wai*-ing (Buddhist greeting with palms held together). We told them they should only *wai* to children under four years old, and to small burrowing animals—and to salute everything else.

The missionary's wife said I was a "delightful disgrace" and I took it as compliment. Then the bill came.

I have a credit card, but as it's my first, I'm really paranoid and I've hidden it under the bed.

So, I pleaded with my friend and said I knew the UN was broke, but I reasoned that another month wouldn't make a damned bit of difference, and also threw in, "Hey, the Americans owe them 7 zillion dollars."

"I know," he said, reluctantly taking out his card. "That's the trouble with wealth."

"What is?"

"You can justify anything when you have it."

Diary of a Sane Man

February 16th: Oxygen tank runs out on way to *The Nation* office *again*! Disembarking from motorcycle, rupture re-breather feed. Co-workers comment I look as miserable as several well-known diseases. Dined on apricot and scallop lozenge; tin of Bulgarian *sauvignon*. It doesn't travel well.

March 1st: Foolishly volunteer to look after neighbour's pets for weekend. Stick insect escapes and eats my palm tree, a dictionary, and the canary. Blood drips, which makes parrot hyperactive.

March 2nd: Give strong worming pills to the rabbit in absent-minded fit. Vet called, sees stick insect clinging to half-eaten curtain. Runs away. At 6 p.m. peed on by tortoise. Half asleep when gorged stick insect falls into bowl of piranhas. Horrific sight. No survivors. Takes three hours to mop up. Berserk parrot insults landlord. What *will* I tell neighbour?

March 3rd: Thoroughly depressed. Disassemble life-support pack and find a false eyelash, a real earlobe, and an apple core stuck in the air-vent. Decide to look for new apartment and new job. Send resume to rival newspaper. Told no vacancies until new millennium. Hear manic laughter in background. Open bottle of cheap vodka apparently made out of ex-communists and mashed yams. Tastes like tractor fuel but does the job. Ring mum in London. Told she's caught in a traffic jam under the English Channel. Good god.

June 20th: Overtaken by 19th empty airport bus this week. Driver smiles, conductor sleeps.

June 30th: Awake from nightmare convinced that Big Mac is a drug dealer and Big Jiew is a hamburger chain.

July 2nd: Told by friend that when you lose who you are, there is only money. Right on cue, baht plunges.

July 4th: Girlfriend goes on diet. Puts me on one. Says foreign food is out. It's grilled locusts for a week. No problem. What do they taste like? "Microwaved beetles," she replies.

August 1st: Prime minister is vague about everything. My toe is stepped on by blind dwarf selling lottery tickets outside Robinson Department Store. Can this mean anything?

August 15th: See photograph of Pol Pot on front page. Looks suspiciously like my Uncle Mac who went missing from retirement home years ago.

August 21st: Baht plummets further, narrowly missing well-dressed beggar on pedestrian bridge on Sukhumvit Road. Astonished, I ask him for a job, as he has more money in his bowl than I do in my pocket. He cackles and asks for foreign currency.

September 1st: Realise, after 30 columns, that Bangkok doesn't build character. It reveals it.

September 11th: Offer the maid 500 baht to immolate interior minister. She shrieks, I freeze. Feel I have insulted her. And I have. Indicates she will be a hero to the Thai people. She *demands* to do it for only 50 baht.

September 29th: Passed by 23rd empty airport bus in four days. Conductor driving. Driver asleep.

October 3rd: On the way to *The Nation* office, upright breaks loose on aural lube filter. Police baffled. Force motor-cycle taxi driver to pay hefty fine and rent two imported gas masks. Weather forecast: visibility—40 metres, temperature—39 degrees, nepotism—91 per cent.

October 10th: Girlfriend down to desired weight. Her hairdryer now weighs more than she does. Asks me to ring modelling agency. I want to call UN for a French parachute drop and World Aid. She is not amused. Serves me one fried locust with missing leg for supper.

October 14th: Realise that while in LA a suntan is considered a cultural achievement, and in London a miracle, in Thailand it seems a distinct disadvantage.

October 19th: Tell girlfriend she looks nice. Thin smile. Passes me sautéed dung beetle. Told someone has found a live tree standing in Burma. Ring office. They are hesitant to run story. Told to thoroughly check sources.

October 22nd: My neighbour hasn't spoken since the loss of half his menagerie. Rabbit still missing. His wife passes me in corridor late at night and hisses, "Even his *bees* don't buzz like they used to."

October 30th: My Thai still hopeless. Insult someone's grandmother while enquiring about price of durian. Accent on wrong syllable. Put card in ATM machine to withdraw 500 baht and receive 17,409 Russian roubles.

November 1st: Find rabbit under repossessed Mercedes! I hug complete strangers. Take animal back to owner. Claims it isn't his. So I eat it. Girlfriend sulks in a corner and sips slug fondue through straw.

November 3rd: Give up smoking, start inhaling pizza. Get offer I can't understand from a girl I can't refuse. Put her card along with the other 2,119 in file marked, "Who the hell *are* all these people?"

November 5th: A stranger knocks and enquires if there are any rooms. Not sure.

"Are there any mice in the building?" he asks.

"No," I reply.

"Oh good."

"The rats ate them all."

November 6th: Ivanov Grobavitch places card in ATM machine in downtown Vladivostok. Receives one kyat, two baht, and a photocopy of a man doing rabbit impersonations in Bangkok. Permafrost devours card. Ivanov takes swig of Siberian lighter fluid and dreams of a beach in Thailand where he can fish for innocence along its polluted waters. But he's a little short of roubles right now.

New Year Anyone?

What *is* it that makes normally polite members of society, who sip sherry and fiddle with delicacies the rest of year, go out and drink four pints of industrial strength tequila, dance naked on tables in front of complete strangers, and even eat the mescal-sodden worm out of the bottle?

Answer? New Year's Eve.

It's the one night of the year when the energy of 12 full moons melt into one, the plot is optional, and the director is called Mr. Excess. It's the night when love is a verb. It's the night that we deliberately go out of control, and do things that are spectacular enough to be worth exaggerating about later.

I was safely back in my cave—having just taken the mammoths out for a late night pee—when the old year was still receiving it's last rites. My genius of a girlfriend was already brilliantly asleep.

Suddenly, her tail twitched, and, dressed only in moonlight and inspiration, she told me to lie down. She then proceeded to wheel out her new invention for the New Year: a homemade, pedal-driven, acupuncture applicator.

"It's only a prototype," she hissed. "Why have you turned pale?"

"Ha! I'm not afraid of *that*!" I replied haughtily. "I've seen more frightening things fall out of a cheeseburger."

Later, the hospital nurses were sympathetic—but giggled just the same—as I lay drugged, hostile, and sore. Down the ward, I heard my girlfriend trying to convince an incredulous doctor to use solar power to regulate my drip-fed morphia. As her voice rose to an elegant shriek—mangling perfectly respectable grammar along the way—stray dogs began to roll over and cover their ears, while sensitive medical equipment blinked on, blinked off, and then blacked out.

I remember the doctor running away, chased by flames. I remember a hissing sound, and I really don't remember anything else.

I came to at home. She was peering at me through a large magnifying glass.

"Facial astrology," she said, as though answering a question. "To ascertain your fortune in the coming year."

It turned out that Saturn was in the ascendant, the moon was somewhere else entirely, and my grammar was shipwrecked on the wrong side of a passing comet.

However, *something* was moving in the right direction because she murmured seductively in my ear, "Is that a work permit in your pocket, or are you just pleased to see me?"

It's hard to make resolutions for a new year when you are full of holes and can't even remember the last one. But under the intense gaze, I promised my pretty little fire-maker that I would:

Look up every word I didn't understand, starting with the word "budget."

When noticing "Suggested Price" labels in Sukhumvit shop windows, immediately go inside and make a suggestion to the person who suggested it.

Keep my passport ready and the engine running.

Buckle my swash more often.

Send car stickers of sympathy to friends in Australia which read, "IF YOU MUST DRINK AND DRIVE, TRY TO DO IT WHEN THE HEALTH MINISTER IS CROSSING THE STREET."

Promise to stop cashing God's cheques because they always bounce.

Then there was a sharp crack as the magnifying glass connected with my skull. "Oh, and to light my baby's fire everyday . . . ," I added quickly.

She hissed me a "Happy New Year," slithered alongside, and handed me her two favourite creations: a scale-massager, and a bottle of uncoiling lotion.

I have to say that when I got to work with them, old acquaintances were completely forgotten.

Jungle Fever

Like many others, I have travelled to seek the rare, the remarkable, and the unrepeatable. My only rule is to avoid going to countries which have had a recent name change. If you hadn't already noticed, Thailand is practically surrounded by them.

Yet here in this enclave of safety, there is the Thailand we want, the Thailand we get, and the Thailand that is. One never really knows quite where one is in this labyrinth of realities, as the one thing reality never is—is, well, *realistic*.

I woke up very early the other day because Pol Pot, my dog, needed to pee and nibble flesh. I had one leg in my jeans and the other in his mouth when the phone rang.

A clipped English accent said, "You look tired."

I knew that voice. It was the voice that had once sent a desperate letter begging me to place a message in a personal column in Bangkok. It had read: "Drunken, insincere extrovert who flies light aircraft, seeks unconventional, tattooed woman with a good body and a sick mind for GIN QUAFFING, passion, and ironing. To share walks, talks, cuddles, and eventually perhaps, a duvet. Own school uniform would help."

I had faxed him immediately with a curt, "No way. Suffer."

It was Hugh and he was back. Sometimes you don't have to travel at all for the unbelievable to come to you.

He wasn't drunk when he arrived at my place later, he was marinated—and crossed the room like a frog on amphetamines: chattering, bulbous, hopping, and quite mad. I was so pleased to see him.

He settled into a large chair and gurgled his gin contentedly. He snoozed, he doodled, and laughed out loud at nothing. He reminded me of me.

What had he been doing the last few years? He remembered being caught in a fierce storm and spending the night lip reading *The Muppets* on Mongolian TV. He had been "up north" in a country where heroin had raised its seductive and dangerous head. He had spent time in India, "a country saturated in prayer," and in the Himalayas, where, "It was so cold you could hear the monasteries sigh with devotion." He had even been in Turkey, where he had taught young men to yoke Armenian tigers with an exhaust pipe.

Then he sheepishly admitted that he'd actually been in town for four days before contacting me. He'd arrived on a Buddhist holiday. The bars were closed. Undeterred, he had roamed the city and found a drink down a dubious alley in a notorious neighborhood—and hours later woke up in a jungle. And *that* was just the beginning.

He came to with his head lodged in the divine fulcrum of a female lap, and its owner was drip-feeding him *Sang Thip* whiskey through a straw. He had glanced down and discovered his toenails were being cut by an entirely different woman. And where were those damn drums coming from . . . ?

Then he suddenly asked me, "Do you remember the famous scene in *Apocalypse Now* when Marlon Brando was staggering around in that Khmer temple, slapping his head and muttering, 'The horror, the horror?'"

"Sure."

"I've always had a problem with it. I mean Kurtz and Conrad never actually *said* what the horror was. I always thought that Brando had inadvertently caught sight of himself in the mirror."

He got up, waddled to the door, gave me a wonderful smile, and said, "Wait till you see my girlfriend."

They came back that night. She was a troubled vision in lipstick with a face like crumpled linen, and a hairdo that had once wrecked a ceiling fan.

Oh well, you can't make appointments with emotion. I thought they were rather well suited; lost in a wet fog of mutual incomprehension.

"She speaks English. Say something darling," he encouraged her.

She hesitated and said, "You can *weach* me on my mobile."

And that was it. The following silence was so deafening you could have heard a dog bark in Burma.

Hugh beamed with pride and said, "She knows the word for wealth in several languages but can't pronounce it in any of them. We're working on it."

Then he asked me how *my* girlfriend was.

"She lives in two worlds. She eats fried locusts for breakfast and is using my computer by noon. Sometimes we drive to a national park. To me, it's a sanctuary of nature. To her, it's a forest brimming with edible wildlife. If we do happen to glimpse a rare animal, I gaze at it in wonder and awe. She points at it and yells, "EAT!!""

"She sounds wonderful. Where did you meet her?"

"In a jungle."

We went out to a restaurant, and after an evening of calm and rather expensive enjoyment, Hugh turned to me over his third brandy and said, "Do you know what pataphysics means?"

I didn't.

"It is the science of imagining solutions."

"That's a perfect description of this city."

"I thought so too. Perhaps we could rename it Patakok."

Maybe, but I think he should ask the owners first.

Made in England

A Thai friend and colleague here at *The Nation* is about to spend a year studying at Oxford University. He is a man of intelligence, charm, and unpolished energy—and he has never been to England.

"Have you packed your velvet smoking jacket?" I asked him.

"My what?"

"Never mind. Some silk cravats should do. By the way, how's your Latin?"

He didn't answer, but wore the expression of a man who has just realised he's left the bath tap on at home. He was ripe for advice, and over the last few days I have tried to explain to him what can be expected from a university that first opened it's creaking, wooden doors in the year 1167.

At the time, King Henry II was on the throne, and the language of the English court was still French—a linguistic hangover from the Norman conquest a century before. I know this because my ancestors were on the beach during the invasion and secured the first French teaching contract for unemployed Saxons. They went broke over the weekend.

Despite the savagery and debauched fun of the Dark Ages, Oxford University was to grow into an environment that would thrive on the oxygen of intelligence and discovery. It continues to do so. My *Nation* colleague may also be astounded to discover that there are still places of learning whose knowledge can never be obtained through the power of purchase.

The German writer, Wolfgang Goethe, said that, "Architecture is frozen music." Wandering around the colleges of Oxford, with their gothic towers, vaulted libraries, and elegant quadrangles, my friend will understand exactly what he meant. The gardens are serene and secret, and the lawns Wimbledon-green and immaculately kept—for turf is the landscape of settled civility.

Oxford is also a place that brims with wonderfully-brained eccentrics. Professors of science may still be glimpsed staggering from chemistry experiments trailing laboratory vapours, while bookish, bespectacled dons can be spotted muttering to themselves in the quad, dipping into their pockets for lines of lost poetry, only to find bits of three-day-old toast—and their glasses. It's the *don* thing.

Oxford professors also tend to be expansive, unpredictable, and slightly dangerous; three fine qualities in a teacher. In the past, some have been burnt at the stake for their beliefs, and one even had the dubious honour of introducing acne into Rhodesia. Yet although each generation of tutors gradually becomes rich in years and dignity, and may well adopt lazy smiles and carry noble paunches, mentally engage them and they move at warp speed.

Many are men of letters, some are men of bottles, but all of them sincerely believe that exams should be treated as a brief interruption to the proper business of education. Real knowledge is not a qualification, it is a process.

The student clientele has certainly changed. Anyone could be sitting next to you—from future dukes, to potential dictators, to beautiful Israeli girls who drive Merkava M3 tanks over the Golan Heights during their holidays. There will also, no doubt, be a smattering of emotionally incontinent fops who clutch teddy bears and, through an absurd right of birth, will end up in the House of Lords—that last infirmary of noble minds. For them, it must be like going home.

I suggested that if he was in any doubt about how to address either a member of staff or a senior student, he should bow slightly from the waist and say, "My liege." Equally, when asked by his tutor if he agrees with what the tutor has just said, and he doesn't have a clue, he should simply nod wisely and reply, "Cunning plan my lord."

Although Oxford is a place where dead languages are taught in preference to living ones, I told him not to fret about his ignorance of Latin. The university has now radically updated it's classical curriculum. It has progressed to the Middle Ages. He might be presented with a Jurassic computer and asked to deal with such challenges as:

A GOBLIN IS RUSHING TOWARDS YOU!

Kill the goblin with an axe.

BUT YOU DON'T *HAVE* AN AXE.

He shouldn't feel too hassled about spelling either. Shakespeare never spelt his name the same way twice, and he never spelt it Shakespeare.

Outside the hallowed halls of learning, Oxford has much to offer. It is a city of old money, pubs, and bicycles, that bulges with student accommodation. It has dormitories and "digs"—and I suggested that as soon as he discovers what that means, he should a get a place of his own. I actually know of some charming cottages in Moreton-on-the-Bog, just outside the city. These 13th-century cottages are small but—wait for it—"have interesting spindle windows with thatched boon lobs on the truncated west mitchet." The terracotta poove vents are a later addition. Admittedly they are dark, even in the light, but he can pick up some spray paint from the 1,500-year-old post office in the village. I advised him to buy the brand which is, "Recommended by seven out of ten mindless vandals."

"What's a mitchet?" he asked.

"You'll know when it leaks."

I also gave him some social pointers. Don't drop litter. Foreigners who drop litter in Thailand are charged 2,000 baht—even though there's not a garbage can for miles. Foreigners who drop litter in England are sent to Australia, nailed to the side of a ship. And these days they have to *pay* for the journey.

Try to be polite to everyone. Manners have little to do with class, though etiquette does. I know working-class people with the most beautiful manners, and upper-class people who behave like yobs. Just like in Thailand, manners are there to get you ahead without anyone noticing what you are doing.

I hope he enjoys the annual Oxford and Cambridge submarine race, while drinking pints of Scruttocks Old Dirigible. And there's a rumour that at the end of the summer, Luciano Pavarotti will be bungy-jumping off the Magdelan College bell tower, naked, while singing that football song. That would be an education in itself.

If he's ever in trouble, he is welcome to visit my mum in Sevenoaks, which, due to a passing storm, is now called Oneoak and is not very well.

She's used to taking in strangers.

Bon chance mon ami.

Opium, Visas, and the Dead

Chiang Mai. Friends and recent visitors said I would hate the place if I returned. It was busier, louder, more commercial. The smiles had vanished, the charm had moved on, and it was definitely the wrong season to go. Temperatures were approaching nuclear proportions.

And they were all wrong. Except about the heat. For nothing had changed except me.

It was a late April pilgrimage—that took me to the place that six years ago, lured me with its *wats* and eccentrics, slow pace and high hills—to discover how time had changed us both.

Messages from the north had filtered down through the years from the odd bar owner, motorcycle rider, and a few traders—all hinting at movement, success, and failure. I had no illusions about returning, but had plenty of expectations on arriving. Must be a family thing.

Lanna and its capital Chiang Mai, is, I believe, a foreign country. The locals, both Thai and foreign, have no time for Bangkok, and can't imagine why anyone would want to live there unless they were forced to.

Leaving the railway station, I was soon heading down the same snoozing *sois* behind Thapae Gate that take devious and compromised routes on their way to nowhere in particular. Pigs loitered in the shadows, chewing on old shoes and dead leaves. I was home again.

There was one survivor from the past, still running a small guest house with a pool. Knowing the language, he could afford to linger with intent. I had always thought he was deaf, but now realised his deafness varied according to what was being said. Six years ago, I used to dream of staying here—yet having now checked in, it wasn't a dream come true, but a nightmare with extra cheese. The showers hissed like vipers but produced no water at all. The toilets were *balkan*. Nothing worked. When the maid came in with the missing soap and towel, she found me standing on a broken chair head-butting the air-conditioner—which sounded like the engine room of the Titanic.

I later heard that the owner had returned one night after one drink too many, and, according to which account you believed, he either drove into the full swimming pool, or dived into the empty one.

Checking out the old haunts, I was crestfallen to discover the gate to the Black Cat Bar firmly chained and bolted. A forlorn air hung over the garden. This had been my centre of operations—for knowledge, laughter, and love; the bar where I had annoyed the dung out of everyone when I gleefully discovered that people actually LIVED in this country without working for a multinational or the UN, and had kept asking, "So what do *you* do?"

I was on a role, and even asked the young, urbane US consul at the time what *he* did.

"Opium, visas, and the dead," he replied.

Seeing my jaw drop, he added, "1,200 tonnes, 90 visas, and about 12 deaths."

Deaths?

127

"A mixture of bike crashes and heart attacks."

It was also the bar where I was persuaded to leave. Not so much for my behaviour, but more to get out and go for the adventure.

To prepare for the greater solo journeys ahead—the Triangle, Mae Hong Song, and Mae Sot—I vividly remember taking the bike up Doi Suthep mountain for a practice run, and then hurtling back down the switchbacks, which resembled a spiritual slalom. Like most English adventurers, I had no fear, no style, and no control.

I learned that one of the owners of the Black Cat had split—leaving behind debt and revenge—and was now back in London driving a cab. Another regular had been shot at by the police, but, according to a local, "They missed, unfortunately." Clearly, his absence was required.

The town wasn't exactly jumping. In the post-*Songkran* let-down and the debilitating heat, the social whirl was basically pond life with a few interesting egos bobbing on the surface. I've seen more action in a dozing amoeba. But then, that's the beauty of this place. The absence of action is a welcome presence.

There were new owners of old bars, and old owners of new ones; raffish, amiable, and interesting drifters who have stayed to became vagabonds with a fixed address—at least for a while. Men who think twice about drinking brandy for breakfast only when pouring a second one. For many, the taste of their produce far exceeds their ambition to sell it. Indeed, many foreigners doing business here look wasted—which is hardly surprising when most of them have spent their entire lives trying to outrun the truth. We are the choices we made.

Down in the extended night market, which still brims with interesting gear, was a gaggle of pensionable Americans dangling deaf aids and asking each other where they lived in the US. The word "operation" recurred frequently.

Most restaurants in Chiang Mai still look inviting and decorous. But the business of catering is to cater, and in some places the food is rarely up to the standard of the furniture. As they say of duff musicals, you come out whistling the set.

McDonalds has finally landed too. No surprise there—just regret. Did you know that the company selected a bright orange colour as being "optimally attractive" for luring customers in—but which would drive them out again after forty minutes? And I always thought it was the food. How silly of me.

I awoke every morning to the sound of two maids giggling outside my room on the verandah. They were watching the eccentric French gay leading his cat on a yellow cord. He was so camp, he winked with a lisp. He always humoured them, and then went downstairs to take his coffee and to dip a lean hand into his wooden box of *Gauloise*. I have no idea what the cat smoked.

The English lolled around the pool in the intense heat, looking pallid, with short cropped hair. It was the *Addams Family* on acid. The Thais don't "do sun," and stared at them, amazed. These world travellers could be seen later in the bar watching mindless violence on video—to "normalise themselves" as one put it. Which says a lot more about the culture they come from rather than the culture they were visiting.

On a table in the guesthouse restaurant was a clumpy, shapeless stone figure of a forgotten Chinese sage. One evening, trying to get away from the gunfire in the bar, I approached, curious. The note next to it read, "12th–13th century. *Ying* Dynasty. Asking price, $25,000." One of the waitresses grinned and asked if I wanted to buy it.

Buy it? I couldn't even lift it.

Then there was an interesting English guy who introduced himself with, "Trust me, I'm a chemist." Which was just fine by me. He'd been in town two days and was hopelessly in love with the cashier in one of the bars. Like your average Labrador dog, he just sat there grinning at her and looking slightly foolish. If he'd had a tail, it would have wagged. To be perfectly honest, I was in love with her too.

He was moving on soon. "So, where to next?" I asked him.

"Heaven," he replied, gazing dreamily at the girl. "Nearly everyone goes to heaven."

Well, maybe, but in my case, I don't see the point. I mean, I wouldn't know anyone. "I think I'd prefer hell," I said.

"What? *Why?*" he said aghast.

"I like the music and I'm used to the heat."

Then I had a glimpse of change. I no longer felt the need to live in Chiang Mai, just the chance to meet those who have.

More 'E' Vicar

At the recent UN drug summit in New York, there was a rumour loose in the convention hall. It was goosing people and biting their ankles. Politicos had been informed that there were individuals taking drugs all over the world, not because they were impoverished and weak, but because they actually enjoyed the experience. Not only that. The vast majority of them were making over 65,000 dollars a year and were turning up for work on Monday.

"It doesn't make sense," said a social worker from Copenhagen.

"Try lighting it from the other end," suggested a drug counsellor from Sydney.

The summit, like all summits, was full of rhetoric.

"Cut the drug supply off at the source." No easy task. Ask Colombia, but don't bother asking Burma. During the eighties, when President Reagan demanded to know why the US was being flooded with cocaine, the Colombian president replied, "Because your country has an insatiable appetite for the stuff." Indeed, Colombian farmers were quite happy to grow coffee. The buzz wasn't as good, but it still kept them awake.

"It's a war on drugs." We've heard that before. Even General Barry McCaffrey, director of the US Office of National Drug Control Policy, was uncomfortable with the metaphor: "A war implies victory. In a war you use violence to destroy an enemy." Quite. One would feel slightly foolish trying to execute a marijuana leaf, or arresting an opium poppy for sunbathing.

In the end, the policy makers spoke a lot, pledged a lot, and failed yet again to address the fundamental question:

Why do people take drugs in the first place?

Human beings and the plants we call drugs—tea, coffee, tobacco, coca, marijuana, opium, and so on—have always lived in symbiosis. For millions, human life is hard and short; drugs offer brief moments outside time and pain. And denied one drug, we find another. Some people become addicted, many do not.

"Reduce the demand." OK, but just how *do* you reduce the demand for drugs? And even if you could, what would you replace it with? Daytime TV? More shopping malls? Political correctness? That's what drives most people to drugs in the first place. Even in the US playground of economic success, an emptiness remains, and the pacifications of consumption are not enough. For many, it's a rebellion against the so-whatness of a consumer-driven society. It's the blandness of it all that drug users seek to escape. Is this *all* there is?

Some people are perfectly happy with what life offers. Some people even like Gorgonzola cheese, Nana Mouskouri, and Belgium. I don't.

Perhaps it's the premise that is all wrong. It shouldn't be a war on drugs, but a war on an increasingly homogeneous world. Organised religion fights a valiant battle but requires too much meditation for those brought up on sound bytes and burgers. In retrospect, it appears that my generation took drugs to find out, to question—rightly or wrongly—whether there was something "else" besides marriage, mortgage, and fog. But then, coming from a country that is built on coal and surrounded by fish, who could blame them?

The following generation took drugs to forget. There's a difference. They were also quick to point out that whatever it was we were seeking wasn't worth it anyway. Time will tell.

Drugs in themselves are not, and have never been, the problem. People are. As composer and musician Frank Zappa once said: "A drug is neither moral or immoral—it's a chemical compound. The compound itself is not a menace to society until a human being treats it as if consumption bestowed a temporary license to act like an asshole."

So. Does a sip of scotch make you an alcoholic?

No.

Does a line of heroin make you an addict?

No, it usually makes you throw up.

But for some individuals, at some point, and at some time, enjoyment spills over into abuse. One isn't enough, and eventually, one is too many.

I have a friend who gave up alcohol because it was bad for his body, so he took up drugs because he thought they were good for his mind. Instead of spending his weekends totally drunk, peeing on historical monuments, and beheading Ronald McDonald statues before he arrived permanently late at his girlfriend's house, he spent his leisure time taking ecstasy and dancing 48 hours non-stop to the Chemical Brothers. Harmless as a kitten.

His brother was amazed at his sibling's new found affection for everyone. But when the vicar came round for an hour on Sunday for tea, the game was up. When the pastor gestured politely with his cup for more, my friend said, "Oh! More 'E' Vicar?"

Another colleague, who scored a first-class honours degree in physics at Sussex University, took three milligrams of pure heroin every day for years. Nobody knew. Nobody even suspected. He appeared bright as a button and went on to teach at a major university in the US. When I met up with him last year, he looked fine. But when I enquired as to what he thought of Stephen J. Hawkins' theories on the universe, he paused for a moment and said, "I don't even understand how his fucking *wheelchair* works."

It seems that drug summits are for those who already have their psychic agenda neatly mapped out. It is attended by people who are scared of those things that don't sit still and pose for an official portrait of reality. It threatens their fabric, and, even worse, their budgets—because the narco-business is now worth an estimated $US700 billion a year. The largest business on the planet. You can't fight that kind of money with money.

So. Should we follow the advice and guidance of those who declare what is legal, harmless, dangerous, and profitable? Sure, why not. But perhaps we should first ask them whether they are a living example of what they expect of other people. Recent events around the region would suggest otherwise.

I was a volunteer drug counsellor in Australia for two years, and during that time came to realise that the lives of the professional psychologists were infinitely more messed up than the lives of those they were counselling. It was enough to turn you to, well, something else.

For centuries drugs have not only healed our bodies, expanded our minds, and provided fun, profundity, and refuge, they have also destroyed us when we could no longer control them. I do not condone drug taking. Practically everyone I know has either lost someone close to drugs, or knows someone who has. My father died at the age of 34 because the right drugs weren't available, while my step-father died at 73 because the right drugs were available but couldn't save him anyway.

My complaint has always been to (and with) those who hold the profoundly childish view of the unknown that, "If it's foreign it must be dangerous." Rubbish. Why is Scotland with it's whiskey any less foreign than Morocco with its *kif*, and Turkey with its opium? All have their qualities and their dangers.

I have also often wondered why it's perfectly alright for an 18-year-old to buy a bottle of Scotch, drink it, beat up his girlfriend, and then get behind the wheel of a car, when it's illegal for someone to take a leaf from a plant and smoke it to bring a few moments of euphoric relief in the privacy of his home.

Because drinking is socially acceptable and marijuana isn't.

So there. Now, what's left that's legal and harmless?

Viagra?

No thanks. I don't know about you, but there's still plenty of lead left in my pencil.

When Kush
Comes to Shove

In the autumn of 1973, on the Greek island of Ios, I readied myself for the long pilgrimage—both within, and without—to the Far East. I had expected to be in Bangkok by Christmas, but I got lost and ended up in the Hindu Kush. I blame it on bad maps and good drugs, but it may well have been the other way around.

I had been comfortably numb on the island, living happily in a goat hut. I was black with tan, glowed with health, and, as the day for departure approached, scared shitless. The only part of the journey that was organised was the promise of a lift to Istanbul in a German car whose owners had already seen better days. After that I was on my own.

With my capital already endangered, I ventured once more to the bar to watch the sun set over the Aegean and listen to Beethoven's "Fifth" from the speakers that were perched on the cliff's edge every evening—to provide the spiritual harmonics of the dusk. Always a centering experience.

Over the years, the overland hippy trail from the West to the East has frequently been ridiculed for both its purpose and intention—most often by those who never attempted it. I have no problem with that. To me, they were fine times and brave days. Some travellers went for cheap dope, others to locate the source of a spiritual doctrine—and to perhaps lose themselves in the hope of finding themselves somewhere else. I was hoping for all three.

A few of these people are now running large companies in Silicon Valley in California, while others are still damping down another chillum in Himal Pradesh. But what the critics forgot was the sheer distance of the odyssey, the casualty rate, and, more importantly, the thundering plunge into the unknown. You can't turn back in the middle of the Iranian desert. It's too late.

For me, it was Afghanistan that was the pivotal and riveting spot. Nice place to pronounce but you wouldn't want to live there. Ask the Russians. Even in late '73, Kabul was a crumbling, turbaned mess. A diplomat's mistress picked me up and took me to the only restaurant in town which still had windows—and immediately regretted it. She kept saying, "*Do* try to look a little wealthier, I have a reputation to maintain."

In the freezing heart of Afghanistan's heroic geography, I remember the ageing truck finally entering the valley of Bamiyan at nightfall—three days after we had left Kabul. The small town announced itself with lights that twinkled from among the rocks, and I heard the only other foreigner on the truck mutter, "Thank *God* there's a God."

The trail had been forged deep into the Hindu Kush, and the vehicle had groaned and swung violently at perilous angles as we were hurled about with every jolt. By the time we arrived, the hot water flasks were cold, the cold water was frozen, and we smelled like old goats. The air was so raw it hurt just *being* in it. Then someone told me it was Christmas day. I was 3,200 kilometres from Bangkok and it was so cold my testicles were the size of peanuts.

Bamiyan is a speck of green in a forbidding landscape—
and is also the furthest point Buddhism ever reached on its
journey west. This grim, mountainous isolation is littered
with abandoned monasteries whose histories seem erased
from time—and although the area is completely desolate,
one feels one is being watched. This is not a place to linger.
This is not a place to be ill or frightened. And one is quickly
reminded of the staggering insignificance of humanity,
which the environment encourages with a mournful, biting,
lunar wind.

Steppe eagles glide high on thermals, lynx and snow
leopards may be glimpsed, and the marmot—from which
you can still catch the bubonic plague—is hunted.

The valley is dominated by a gigantic, sixty-metre
standing Buddha hewn out of the rock face which towers
over the settlement below. Being a Christian in an Islamic
land, and experiencing this lonely and powerful outpost of
Buddhism, felt like being on a spiritual fault line. It is not a
place of answers, but of questions. It's difficult to get to—
which could well have been the intention; a secret valley
housing the open heart of Buddhism with it's compas-
sionate, brave, and intelligent message.

The cliff-face is still honeycombed with small caves and
passageways which are covered with wall paintings that tell
the tale of an attitude that can eventually both help and
liberate. Over the centuries, as travellers approached from
the west via Herat, the first glimpse of this statue would
have suggested the end of one world and the beginning of
another—as the looming figure represents a gateway to a
whole different option.

The Buddha no longer has a face and the valley is long
empty of Buddhists. The Mongolians—known as the people
of "The Blue Wolf"—under the command of Genghis Khan,
literally swept through here like a carnivorous plague with
a taste for destruction. His vast, horse-backed army was

preceded by the stench of death, borne by an east wind, and followed a week or so later by the thunder of half a million hooves.

That Christmas night, under the faceless Buddha, under the icy celestial canopy, I huddled next to the available humanity for warmth. As I leafed through the third chapter of *The Tibetan Book of the Seriously Ill,* while chewing on a fistful of dried goat curd, I started to laugh. Maybe I hadn't reached Thailand, but I had arrived at the far outpost of her religion. What an entry. What a present.

Today, 25 years later, this lonely Buddhist sentinel is threatened again—and the question is not so much whether the Taleban army will or won't destroy the statue, but why on earth they would *want* to? Does a 2,000-year-old carving pose such a threat to their strict and severe intentions? Maybe it does. Give a man a pocketful of bullets and his soul takes a vacation.

Last night, I dreamed I was at a conference being held in a huge tent in a vast desert. The assembly were debating whether to raise a Sufi army to protect this ancient Buddhist signpost.

It was a heated and noisy affair. Wise-looking men with long white beards huddled with Buddhist representatives from Sri Lanka, India, and beyond. Time was running out and the Taleban leader wasn't even answering his expensive mobile phone. What to do?

It was decided that the Sufis were now too evolved for violence, and would not heed a call to arms. It was then suggested that perhaps the karmic reaction to the inevitable destruction of the Buddha would bring forth the long awaited heir to Genghis Khan—who would then invade Afghanistan for old times sake.

Sage-like heads nodded in agreement. The descendant of Khan was indeed alive, and what's more, could be found easily.

The idea was picking up energy, and it was soon agreed that not only would the heir of Khan make mincemeat of the Taleban Hell's Angels, he could, while he was up and about and feeling frisky, perhaps be persuaded to take on SLORC the following week in Burma—which everyone reasoned would only entail a pleasant afternoon's work. It was agreed he would be paid handsomely for the overtime. In return, the newly-crowned Khan would allow the Buddhist statue to be rebuilt, to replace the face his ancestor hacked off eight hundred years ago.

And so it was settled.

A good-looking monk then suggested that a call should be placed to the Taleban, and to leave the decision on the answering machine. Everyone laughed, and the call was placed.

As I awoke, I swear I could still hear the click of worry beads being worked frantically by a man wearing a turban in a dim cave in a troubled land.

Any Which Way but Up

I spend a lot of time on motorbikes owned by other people. In this city and in this traffic I prefer, pervertedly perhaps, to put my life in someone else's hands. And I pay for it.

One reason is the death count of friends, which currently stands at six. It may be seven, but when I went to see an acquaintance in the ICU at the Police Hospital, I couldn't recognise him. His head had been shaved, and his dome looked like a map of Mars criss-crossed with tyre tracks left by some Pathfinder probe. He had no ID and I had no idea. And a doctor looked away.

Another reason is the horror stories from those who own a bike in someone else's name, and then get hit by someone entirely different. Unless you own a small country somewhere, it is always the foreigner's fault. Insurance? There is no insurance in Thailand, and if there is such a thing, you'll be receiving your pension before you get a payout. Solution? Crisp notes in a greased palm. The lubricants of justice.

Upcountry it is different. More room, less people. I spent months in the early nineties biking alone through the glorious steep greenery of Northwest Thailand. It was one of the main reasons I came back to live here—although oddly, I have never returned to the place that made me want to.

And I have been lucky—so far. Just a couple of minor calamities. Completely mesmerised by the lonely beauty surrounding the road from Chiang Mai to Mae Hong Song, I failed to see the large pothole until it was too late. Although the pitch of my voice has not changed, I very much doubt if I will ever father children in this lifetime. Thank God no one was looking.

In Pai, another *incidenté*. There, I laid the blame on the beauty of its women. My gaze lingered a smidgen too long on the face of a market girl which was blessed with God's brushstroke, and I clipped a parked motorcycle—which toppled onto the next one, and the next, and the next, setting off a chain of collapse and embarrassment that saw a dozen bikes go down like pinballs. Bop-bop-bop. An old man on a bicycle was so excited by this spectacle, he lost his own balance and ploughed into a hedge behind a fruit stall, scattering squawking chickens and excited children. I fled and hid and laid low, and then slinked away under the cover of darkness.

I have a deal with a rider who takes me to *The Nation* office every day. I trust him because I have to. He's fast but he's safe. And boy, do we zip. Weaving between the battered buses and bitumen galleons of Bangkok, I've often encountered stares of resentment mixed with envy from those entombed in cars. They may have mobiles, but I am more mobile than them. It's true what they say: the wheel enabled man to get ahead, until he got behind it.

And there are rewards besides the convenience of speed. I've picked up three wing mirrors this year so far. One is a beauty. We were passing a massive limo. Inside were herds of leather and flocks of wool. The car was so big you wouldn't so much park it, as dock it. Suddenly, my right hand, acting without orders—I really can't explain it officer—shot out and snatched the wing mirror. It was the catch of the day.

I have often wondered where Thai people learn to drive. Have you ever seen an 'L' plate, or a "Please slow down, driver under instruction" sticker on the back of a car? An American on his first visit to the UK thought an 'L' plate meant the car was being driven, not by a learner, but by a leper.

But I am sure of one thing. There is no such thing as an accident. It is a sequence of events. Mine started by using a different rider, who immediately made a perfectly casual u-turn outside the World Trade Center in the middle of 70,000 cars hurtling in the opposite direction. Then he nonchalantly sped up the impossible corridor that is Sukhumivit Road, passing in quick succession, Le Meridien President Hotel, which still looks like it was hit by an Exocet missile, the Central Department Store, which appears to be draped in a death shroud, and the walls of privilege surrounding the British Embassy. Soon, we were zooming past the empty condominiums that have become the hasty gestures of permanence—and that's when the driver overshot the entrance to the *soi*.

I yelled, "Back!"

And he yelled, "*Who?*"

And then a taxi hit us from behind. Its driver not only fled the scene of the crime, he didn't even bother stopping for it. Hit and run in action. In the next few seconds, there was blood on the tyres of his taxi going east, and a crash helmet in the hands of a kid going west.

The vehicle had clipped our back wheel, and we were airborne without instructions, spinning without control. Dimensions became confused. The landscape was wandering all over the place, yet hadn't moved at all, and suddenly there was the ground—accelerating towards us like a bad cartoon. The sudden crunch of human cargo is like the sound of an apple hitting concrete. Thunk.

A neck can snap like a candle. A knee can crack like a nut. But neither did. I just thought that sounded good.

Still, voyeurs gathered, under the feeble guise of concern. The bike lay on its side, still twitching and screaming revs. It sounded like a cat giving birth to a BMW. The bike rider was shaken and gashed, and he winced theatrically as a policeman—a "whole policeman" as they say in Nigeria—sauntered up, surveyed the scene, asked for a cigarette, and split.

I checked all my circuits—which seemed to be humming—stood up, and promptly keeled over as the right ankle gave way. That's when the kid stole the helmet. Quick in thought and fleet of foot. I was at once angry, and then impressed. He reminded me of me, the little tyke.

My bits are healing fast, but if anyone should happen to spot a two-foot urchin with a helmet ten sizes too big still running towards Burma, let me know will you? I'd like a quiet word with him. As for the taxi driver, he'll be easier to find. Because his left wing mirror is missing. If he wants it, he can come and get it. It's here on my table, along with all the others.

Unplugged
and Unstamped

It is a fact that much of humanity lies in the archives of bureaucracy. The fact that we are all being logged-in and stored in a tiny chip is simply a change of style, not intent.

Yet behind the bleeps and digits, and the bells and gongs, there lurks the civil servant in whom, somewhere, there lies the remnants of a human being. We have all met one—but only when we needed to. It is the man behind the desk, the relic of a cleric, the faceless bureaucrat who is professionally indifferent to change.

I was returning an application form that was so long it made the Old Testament look like a *haiku* poem—and I was already depressed in anticipation of failure when I walked into the office. The only person in the dingy, grim, metallic-coloured room made no attempt to rise from his chair, but with an ingenious movement of his hands, gave the impression that he was sitting down after already having done so. It was quite brilliant.

The clerk behind this desk was a man of signatures and forms, and flow charts and flip charts—in duplicate, triplicate, and even quadruplicate. A man of rubber stamps for approval, disapproval, and referral. He took my passport to examine it, prod it, question it, doubt it, and—I sincerely hoped—make very close friends with it.

When he walked to a filing cabinet, I noticed his legs were of unequal length. He appeared to be going downhill and uphill at the same time, and, at one point, even sliding to the side.

With an irredeemable haircut, he was overdressed in indescribable garments—which greatly enhanced his civic position but said nothing about the man inside at all. Bunches of medals but no scent of battle. All hat and no rabbit. There was no feature on his face that you could you rest your eyes on for reference. It screamed bland, and lacked emotional weight.

His furious stamping and leafing of forms were the only signature of his personality. He seemed enmeshed in a hundred forgotten policy documents of vital importance.

He was also a man who could turn a straight question into an insistent answer. "England," he said, as he slowly turned the stained pages of my passport.

"Yes, England."

"You here."

"I know," I said quietly. It sounded more like an admittance of guilt, rather than a simple and obvious statement of fact.

"What your work?"

"I shout at foreigners."

"Why?"

"To learn them to speak English as she is spoke."

He looked at my application and began to slowly shake his head. He placed the form carefully to one side and then very slowly unsheaved a leaf from a ream of paper as his profession required—being famously obsessed with time to the detriment of motion.

"Write this way. Now."

When it came to the military service question I wrote, "Exempt." The next question was, "Reason for exemption?" This was tricky. I was tempted to write, "Because we won," but quickly saw the foolishness of this imperial arrogance and simply wrote, "Still trying."

I handed him the form, at which point his unusually large hands shot out from his tight sleeves, hotly pursued by enormous cuffs to receive it. He surveyed the form as if it was a map of Iraq.

"Why you want stay here?"

"To retire."

"You too young."

"As a student?"

"You too old."

This was not going well. Not only had I turned up in the wrong language, I had turned up at the wrong age as well.

I was considering euthanasia when the phone on his desk rang. He let it ring four times so the person at the other end would be delighted that someone was there. "Bastard," I muttered.

He spoke into the phone, and suddenly his face had character. It portrayed the look of a man who'd only just realised he'd left his wallet at the Yokohama Karaoke and Hookers Club the previous evening. Suddenly I felt much better.

Then a really extraordinary thing happened: he blushed.

Civil servants don't blush. And gorillas don't purr.

He came back to the desk, whipped out some paper, jammed it into his typewriter, and pecked furiously at the keys. Someone, something, some*where* had made him angry—and I knew then that I was doomed. I knew my entity was gone, and I was about to become an unwanted comma in an unknown file.

He ripped out the paper, clipped it, stamped it, punched it, and then tore it up.

"I solly. Bring your bassboot back tomorrow," he said with cold apology.

Then he turned his back on me and hobbled to the left towards his filing cabinet which was over on the right. And I walked straight out of the door.

Remember. Nothing of value comes overnight.

Resting between Challenges

On a recent trip to London, I discovered there'd been an astounding change. On a clear day in our neighbourhood, you could now hear the car theft alarms from nine streets away.

This is amazing. For when I lived there, there *were* no car alarms. There were only about three cars, and if we spotted someone trying to steal one, we simply unleashed whatever animal was awake, which then limped off after the idiot in a frenzy of indifference.

I also discovered the new generation. My three nephews are now tall, have very short hair, and look slightly menacing. They are at that awkward and pivotal stage of late adolescence; they have nice girlfriends but appalling zits. They have imperatives rather than memories, and suffer from everything except experience.

The youngest nephew never really gets completely dressed because he's never up long enough to make it worthwhile. I love him. He somehow inherited an unambitious dog which, like its owner, is now a very mixed up animal. To call it a dog is flattery. It isn't a dog, it's just a bundle of filth on a lead. The only exercise either of them gets is the weekly, fifty metre walk to the post office to pick up his welfare cheque. It's the most exhausting thing they do all week.

I think they are both quite innocent, for they seem prepared to lose their virginity to anything that has a pulse. Must be a family thing.

The middle nephew is training to do voice-overs for commercials. He gets instructions like, "More smile in the voice please." His weekends are spent surrounded by very expensive stereo equipment while ingesting very expensive substances. He would like to be a smuggler. He dreams of driving through the Channel Tunnel with a full truckload of looted ostriches and gangling apes. His father thinks it's time they discussed career options.

The eldest is typical of a certain type of London "yoof"— peaceful until provoked, dangerous when attacked, and elusive until hungry. He is also the most individual of the three. He has the courage to be lazy but actually washes his own clothes by stamping on them in the shower. He is unemployed but prefers to call it, "Resting between challenges."

They took me out for a drink. Rising from the London Underground, we walked to a pub. There were beggars in front of us, muggers behind us, and the sex workers were closing in on all sides. In the pub, I met their friends, who all had Cockney accents and seemed to glory in their own incoherence. Over pints of cider they grilled me about Bangkok.

"Are the girls beautiful uncle?"

"Don't call me uncle. Yes."

"Do you have to pay?"

"Listen. People sleep together for all sorts of reasons everywhere. Why shouldn't money be one of them?"

"Can we come and stay?"

"Well guys, I only have a small place."

Crushed by their bearhugs of farewell at Victoria Station, I went to see my mum in Kent. It's another England. It's another century.

It was wickedly cold. Spring was ten days old yet your spit froze before it hit the ground. She lives in a village that is a thousand years old. The elite longbowmen of Henry V's army once practiced on the hill behind her house on their way to Agincourt for the Anglo-France Tour of 1415. When good, they could pierce a man's heart from four hundred yards—just ask the French. They even had groupies.

In the village next to the Saxon church are the good offices of the eminent lawyers, Gimlet, Firkin, and Groat. Nobody has been seen entering the front door since King Ethelred the Untogether died in the ninth century.

I was grilled about Bangkok. "It's just Hong Kong with manners Mum," I said.

"How are your nephews? I'm worried about them."

"Relax, they're just growing up. By the way, have you ever eaten ostrich?"

"Good God no, I've never even seen one."

"It's no matter. I just heard there might be some available, that's all."

"Garden's looking great Mum."

"Air Raid Live Tonight! Admission Free for Prisoners"

On January 2nd 1943, five Australian men who had been working in the tin mines at Yala in Southern Thailand, were brought under Japanese guard into the internment camp that had been hastily constructed on the playing fields behind Thammasat University in Bangkok.

The Australians were exhausted. Three of them were still lame from wounds. They'd had a very bad time of it down south, and a number had been killed. They now joined over three hundred Commonwealth internees made up of traders, university teachers, insurance men, lawyers, and their wives and children.

The new experience of confinement soon brought out the best and the worst in people. Those civilian internees who had cruised through their office days in Bangkok in a crapulous haze of dry martinis, were now sober for the first time in years. They lost weight, began to read, and organised drama societies and lecture evenings. A few, who weren't used to picking up anything heavier than money, refused to join in any activity in the camp, and remained aloof, separated by their own arrogance, no doubt feeling that they were too special to have to do anything either for themselves or for others. They were ignored, and withdrew into a spiteful silence. Nothing changes!

Although everyone in the camp believed in the need for freedom, many understood the greater importance for order. In the tight and crowded circumstances one without the other was dangerous. As it was, there were marital affairs, personality clashes, and furious arguments over the hierarchy of command—and children saw adults under stress at close quarters; always a valuable education. With so many people to organise, committees were established to handle the sleeping arrangements, first-aid classes, sporting activities, sewer duties, the cooking, and the complaints. It had all the makings of some insane tropical soap opera.

To those outside of Thailand at the time, Bangkok was a mere backwater in the furious theatre of a global war. Yet these internees had a ringside seat when the first major Allied bombing raids began over the city on January 8th 1942. They were to continue for the next three and a half years.

From the diary of an English trader after a raid in April 1943: "As the alarm sounded some idiots in one of the camp buildings started to smoke, and after a warning, were shot at by the guards ... next day we discovered that the raid had hit Assumption College, a clinic at the end of Silom Road, and a row of shops on Jawarat Road. There were many Chinese casualties."

Later on in the war, waves of American Super Flying Fortresses would come howling and thundering "a mere 600 feet above the river following its curve and midnight glisten to the bridges and railyards at Lopburi. Many a hole was made in our mosquito nets when the ack-ack guns finally spoke . . ."

By which time, it appears, the bombers were already over another province, if not another country.

A former Archbishop of Canterbury once said that, "Cricket is merely organised loafing." He may be on to something there. At the camp, teams were patched together that consisted of men and women from countries as far apart as Uganda and New Zealand.

A young Canadian who was politely asked to play at 'silly mid-off,' picked up a stump and threatened the umpire—a matronly, middle-aged English woman from Devon.

Bad idea.

She coolly told him to, "Play where you're told, or you'll be moved to 'square-leg'—and may I remind you, I have a bottle of Scotch that's older than you." At which point he "jumped into the river and swam off in the direction of Thonburi in a frightful rage, waving the cricket stump above his head, cheered on by two grinning solicitors from Ceylon holding plates of sandwiches."

The Thai guards gulped once and blinked twice, but didn't shoot. I wonder what the Archbishop would have thought of that.

At the war's end, the last entry in the trader's diary is not his own, but from a survivor recently liberated by the Allies from the Thai-Burma railway in September 1945:

"Two hundred of us dressed in a queer assortment of garments dropped from relieving aircraft, filed noisily into a large hangar at Don Muang airport. Then an astonishing thing happened. All fell silent as we caught sight of a table in a corner with tea-urns and mugs on it. Standing there, smiling, was a pretty English girl with long fair hair sweeping in a wave over her neck, dressed in a crisp summery outfit. Two hundred toughs, clad like scarecrows, were hushed by the sight, and many were visibly affected. She signalled to us to file past to receive tea and sandwiches, and we did so quietly and even shyly. An elderly, unshaven private immediately in front of me, when asked if he would like sugar, murmured with genuine feeling, the old hack-neyed reply, 'Oh Miss, if you just put your finger in it, it will be sweet enough.' He stared at her in a dog-like way, and stumbled past, blinded by her presence."

By the way, the English do not watch cricket, they study it. To find out how people perform while loafing about.

Soup, Debt, and Effort

Golf. I have always had a realistic suspicion that men who play golf can no longer get it up anything which is close to them in the dark, and therefore *have* to get it into something which is far away from them in the light. The cost is about the same. And do you know why golf is called golf?

Because all the other four letter words were taken.

And why do these people strive so hard for a "handicap" when it's perfectly obvious to everyone—except, perhaps the Ape People of the Indus—that they have a very serious one already?

I've only played this absurdity once. It was on a small island off the west coast of Australia which is inhabited by giant rats called quokkas. The greens were grassless—no doubt munched by these prehistoric throwbacks—and it was like playing on the moon.

"How was your weekend?"

"Great. I played lunar golf surrounded by huge rodents."

"Are you *nuts*?"

Yes. What's more, my friend and I were on the ninth hole discussing career options, as usual, when the lightening struck him; 66 billion volts. Zapped straight through his body.

He sizzled. He was barbecued. He was well-done.

He emerged from this cosmic alarm call with neither his pants nor his putter. His face was blackened and there were little explosions coming off his charred clothing that fizzed, popped, and snapped. Because of the intense heat, a small tablet involuntarily launched itself skyward from his shirt pocket, leaving a trail of exhaust behind it. He just stood there crazed and blasted, watching this pharmaceutical rocket disappear into the clouds.

"I was saving that for my birthday," he said, and began weeping softly.

"Are you OK?" I yelled from behind a bunker a hundred metres away.

"Never felt better mate," he said suddenly brightening. "In fact, I've just made a career decision. I'm going to open a restaurant in Bangkok."

"What? Are you *nuts*?"

"Yes."

"But you have no experience."

"I do now," he said, and collapsed in shower of sparks.

I was there at the opening a year later. It was crowded as only a small shophouse in Klong Toey can be. It was a bit of a slum, but even slums look better at night.

He now had a limp—and lightbulbs would surge with sudden power whenever he passed—but otherwise he appeared to be as happy and dysfunctional as ever.

It could hardly be called a restaurant. It was more of a kitchen brimming with soup, debt, and effort. Maybe they are the same thing.

"Who's here?" I asked.

"Everyone except the police! And they'll be here any minute," he said over his shoulder, sweating and laughing while carrying a stack of half-finished plates back to the kitchen.

He was already heavily in debt, and hadn't collected a single baht for a meal yet. There was a telegram nailed to the kitchen wall from one very unhappy investor which read:

"BASTARD, REPEAT BASTARD. ABUSIVE LETTER FOLLOWS."

He was very proud of it, and was thinking of having it framed—while I was wondering what could possibly be in the letter to come.

"So what are you serving?" I asked.

"I thought we'd start with the bison's lung."

"Jesus! No *wonder* the plates aren't finished!"

"No, no, they loved the lung. I think it was the goat's scrotum that may have been a bit too rich."

And that was just the appetiser. The main course was a gastronomic Hiroshima. The meat, whatever it was, was burnt beyond recognition, and the vegetables, although unscathed by fire, were all decomposing through sheer boredom and neglect. The queue for the single toilet was ominous.

"How much do you have to pay the, uh, you know, each month?"

He looked at me with pity. "Listen, corruption is not an obstacle to opening a business here, it is the lubricant."

A Japanese couple entered and sat down smiling, perhaps expecting the karaoke would begin at any moment. My friend walked over to take their order. They didn't understand a word he was saying but nodded a lot and took a photograph of him.

He yelled towards the kitchen, "Two giant rats, medium rare, and a bread roll! Oh, and turn the radio on, they may want to sing . . ."

Position Wanted:
Anywhere but Here

It has been my experience that no one is truly more themselves when either struck down by illness, or threatened with danger. That's when the qualities reveal themselves.

And that's when things get interesting, because the reactions of people we think we know can often be the opposite of what we expect of them when the unexpected arrives unexpectedly.

There are countless tales of characters normally upfront, confident, and reliable, who were the first to split at the merest hint of smoke or danger, and, what's more, were seen elbowing blind nuns and small children out of the way in the rush.

But then the painfully shy computer dweeb in the corner who never said anything to anyone for two years, was spotted *repeatedly* dashing back into some inferno, miraculously emerging every 15 minutes with armfuls of singed babies and little old women clinging to his back.

So, if individuals pitch and yaw under stress—and by doing so, reveal themselves—can the reaction of an entire city under threat reveal its character? You bet it can.

The defining moments in London's history that signalled its change and development usually involved wit, violence, ignorance, plague, and, luckily, a sharp writer who got it all down before he was either consumed by the event, or arrested for organising it.

As a result, these turning points were recorded, and eventually embedded in the national character—whether 'Inglish skool kids' today are hip to it or not.

So, for the Bangkok man who once had a corner on the market, but now has a market on the corner, here is a sobering, yet hopeful tale of how Londoners reacted to, er, a couple of minor problems.

In the bitterly cold winter of 1664-5, the River Thames in London froze solid. Those who depended on it's flow for a living either starved or turned to other means for sustenance, the favourite choice being mugging. Nothing changes! Yet they could hardly complain—as the icy conditions were preventing the spread of something far worse and truly gruesome. Plague.

And not for the first time. In the medieval alleys where roaches strutted and beggars scuttled, the Black Death had been a rapacious gatecrasher for years.

Just before Christmas 1664, the *Parish Bills of Mortality* (which covered Greater London and its population of almost half a million people) showed that 68,596 died of the plague between December 1663 and December 1664. That's 15 per cent of the population of London. In a year.

And it was just the beginning. That winter, 1664, was followed by an abnormally hot summer, and this new wave of plague—whose visual symptoms were soft black swellings which first appeared on the throat or under the armpit, and were almost certain signs of death—matured into a full blown epidemic.

No one was safe or immune. Priests abandoned their parishes, and then the rich their servants, in a massive emigration from London of those of "birth, position, and wealth."

Over the next 15 months, more than 100,000 Londoners were to die. The worst month was September 1665, when an average of 1,500 people wheezed a last painful breath every single day.

Death must surely have come as a relief. Euthanasia would have made a killing.

Buildings in the crowded 160 hectares of the inner city were mostly small, cramped, ill-constructed, and with sanitation so primitive it was said that with a westerly wind, London could be smelt downriver at Tilbury, nearly 20 miles away. Just being there would make you retch at the stench, or die from the inhalation.

Even CNN would have been hard pressed to cover the numbers: "Death coming to you live here in Hyde Park, and Kensington and, *geez*, here in Blackfriars as well. To hell with it, it's back to you Atlanta. This is Chuck Beaver in London and I'm not feeling too good myself."

Graveyards quickly filled with layers of bodies buried only centimetres beneath the earth. The air was foul and putrid. Pits were then dug in any vacant patch of earth, lined with quicklime, and filled with corpses. Those who could get out of the city did—many taking the plague with them.

Fear became panic. Some who found the warning signs on their skin stood crying and roaring at their windows— at either God, Satan, or both at once—while relatives restrained many by lashing them to their beds with ropes or chains. Some Londoners, either smart or just fortunate, took refuge on the abandoned hulks in mid-river that were only afloat because they lacked the decency to sink. A high proportion of these people survived.

The grave diggers, often drunk, and working in shifts around the clock, couldn't keep up. Some corpses lay stacked like wax figures in the streets for two or three days.

Then an order went out to kill all the cats and dogs in the city—on the theory that they might be spreading the disease. It was estimated that collectively, 240,000 were killed within days. These animals, along with the dead pigs and horses, quickly swelled up and burst under the summer sun. With their removal, the *real* carriers of the plague—fleas from the Norwegian brown rats which came to the city on trading ships—multiplied, got busy, went straight for the human jugular, or happily settled for a warm furry spot.

It was frighteningly evident that no one had a clue as to what was causing the sickness, let alone how to deal with it. There is a resonance here somewhere.

Overcrowding in "pest houses," as hospitals were called, was soon so great that visitors had to walk *across* the beds instead of around them. Corrupt doctors took a calculated risk in remaining in the city, and they compounded potions from pepper, urine, and salt. Others sold amulets or undertook purging or crude surgery. Soon, these men were among the richest left in London.

Damage control laws flew fast. All lodgers, visitors, guests, and relatives who usually stayed with householders in London were ordered to leave; they could die wherever they pleased, as long as they did so outside the city limits.

Good idea, but six months too late. By now, country towns and villages throughout England had posted guards with firearms to turn away all who might have come from the capital. These refugees from disease were constantly pelted with rocks and manure wherever they sought sanctuary.

Back in the city, many of the great houses had contained fifty servants or more, and gangs of these newly unemployed now roamed the streets looting abandoned houses and robbing the few pedestrians that were still well enough to *be* one.

In desperation, the government then decided on something truly draconian. Each house in which the plague was found was to be slammed shut with all the residents inside, infected or not, for forty days, and marked with the sign of the plague—a crude red cross smeared on the door. If they lived, they were let out—if they didn't, the house was burned to the ground.

Invariably, entire families were left to die in appalling conditions. Imprisoned, all they could do was hang banners from their windows which read, "Lord have mercy on us."

He would have to; few living things would go near them. Hundreds simply starved to death. Call me what you will, but God can be a real shit sometimes.

All the while, countless bonfires were set in the narrow lanes to purge the air. Church bells tolled, and the only movement in the fetid streets was the carts carrying the dead.

King Charles II, who had remained in the city to keep up morale as long as he intelligently could, finally left on June 29th, 1665 for the relative safety of Hampton Court, two hours by horse to the west of the city. A wise decision, and, in retrospect, nicely timed, for in the first week of August the death toll increased to 2,020 on one single day.

By late summer, many grave diggers and "dead cart drivers" were infected; until then they had appeared curiously immune. Some died at the reins of their carts, which, stacked with corpses, moved on aimlessly at the whim of the horses. Imagine.

Finally, by December 1665, partly with the onset of cold weather, the number of casualties began to decline, and in the New Year, the exhausted city began to show some signs of life. A shaky confidence emerged.

Just nine months later, a little before 2 a.m. on the night of September 2nd, 1666, a workman in Farriner's bakery in Pudding Lane, right in the heart of the city, smelled smoke and aroused the household. The baker, his wife, and their child hurried over the rooftops to safety, but their maid, too timid to follow, was burned alive. Helped by a strong wind, the flames spread quickly. The parish constable arrived, took in the situation, and ran to wake up the Lord Mayor of London, Sir Thomas Bloodworth—who thought it not worth his attention and went back to bed, grumpily observing, "Pish! A woman might piss it out!"

Come the dawn, three hundred houses, several churches, and half of London Bridge had burned down. Riverside warehouses were exploding in the intense heat, causing their stores of oil, tallow, wine, and spirits to spew into the river. People buried their possessions in their meagre backyards, if they had one, and fled. Thousands of pigeons, reluctant to leave their homing perches, fluttered about, and in their hesitation were incinerated. By nightfall a huge arch of fire could be seen crowning the city. By daybreak the Royal Exchange was a smoking ruin.

That morning, French, Dutch, and "Papists" were arrested—for their own protection—as rumours grew of a foreign plot.

Within two days, two thirds of the city was gone. Ninety-seven churches, including the original St. Paul's Cathedral, were now a memory. In addition, 13,200 houses in 117 parishes were destroyed. Wherever the fire was put out, it flared up elsewhere. Munitions experts from the English navy were brought in to blow up entire streets in the fire's path—and *just* managed to stop the flames reaching the Tower of London, where the entire armed forces magazine was kept. King Charles II, right back in the action, was seen helping the soldiers, sleeves rolled and hauling buckets.

By the end of the day, the worst was over, and that evening thousands of exhausted Londoners camped like refugees outside their own city. The King rode out to speak to them, quelled their fears of a foreign plot, and promised to provide them with bread.

Despite the King's words, Robert Hubert, a Frenchman, later confessed to setting fire to the baker's shop and was hanged—his head left on a spike on Blackfriars Bridge for all to see. Only the German bombing during World War II outdid the great fire in it's ferocity, which completely laid waste the inner city.

Was London's true character exposed?

Sure. All of it. Plus luck, which *always* has fun in disaster areas. For thousands of other Londoners though, survival was simply the triumph of enthusiasm over brains.

Were any lessons learned?

Well, for all their arrogance, the English are a tight-pored and tough-grained race, and know an opportunity when they see one. It wasn't long before they realised that what the fire had done was fry the rats, zap whatever goop of death they were carrying, and had burned down many of the rotten wooden houses that harboured it.

Although somewhat charred and bewildered, they rebuilt the city, and soon took a great liking for sending people overseas to run other peoples' cities—quite often whether they were asked to or not.

Well, it seemed much safer than staying at home.

A Cheque in
the Right Direction

The first time I saw Carolyn Tarrant, she was handing a plate of sandwiches to two beaming Nigerians at the 1995 Ploenchit Fair, while standing between a Ferris wheel and a Gurkha.

But I may have been mistaken, as two other people swore it was the British Ambassador's wife. Yet it hardly seemed to matter at the time; the afternoon was fading and things were getting just a tad hazy.

My eventual interview with the lady who *is* the face and name behind the United Kingdom Committee for Thai Charities (UKCTC) annual fair, was just as vague—involving two cancellations, three venues, and four meetings, the last of which took place at her sprawling house tucked away somewhere off Sukhumvit Road.

"Don't mind the dogs," she called from upstairs, while I tip-toed around a pack of growling mongrels, who bore all the signs of misspent youth and uncertain heritage. "Ignore them. Don't even try to be friendly because it's a waste of time."

Which was just fine by me. Dogs? What dogs?

Interviewing Carolyn Tarrant is a thoroughly rewarding and sharp experience, for here is person who thrives on the challenge of creating solutions. Having good intentions is simply not enough. She is also an absolute wizard at getting you to part with your money, while at the same time making sure that you enjoy the giving—even if you're not quite sure where the giving is going.

"It's the twinkling blue eyes and the smile. Gets them every time," says Carolyn with twinkling blue eyes and a smile. "I learned that from Rose Taylor who was running Ploenchit Fair when I first came to Bangkok in 1978. It was a good lesson."

It certainly was, because I suddenly noticed my hand was withdrawing a 100-baht note from my shirt pocket.

"But to reach the standard that the UKCTC have now," continued Carolyn smoothly, casually taking the note from my hand which, by now, had stretched right over to her, "I had to learn patience, and to learn that, I had to understand the Thai way."

That was 19 years ago. Since then, and largely due to her own persistence and energy, the revenue from the Ploenchit Fair has increased from a creditable 800,000 baht in 1978, to a staggering 5.1 million baht in 1996. Every baht has gone to a wide range of charities who haven't actually seen any of it at all.

Really? And why is that?

"Because we don't give cash," says Carolyn. "And that's the beauty of it."

Indeed it is. For the whole emphasis of the UKCTC is to help people to help themselves, with projects which will benefit communities over a long period of time. Does your village school need a new roof? Is your remote hamlet in need of two hundred ducks? A rice bank? Medical equipment? Does your orphanage need musical instruments? Send the details, the reasons, and who it's going to help. No cash, no middleman, just results.

"Every January, the UKCTC committee meets to divide the money among the charities. It usually works out anywhere between 50,000 to 200,000 baht, and we help and monitor every step of the way. The books are open, there are no secrets."

Hearing Carolyn warm to her work instinctively makes you want to raise your game, or at least get the ball back over the net from time to time. The effect is both strenuous and exhilarating, and reminds me of whoever it was who said, "Lead, follow, or get right out of the way."

She is also living, dynamic proof that charity work is not for the meek. To give well and effectively takes integrity, staying power, loads of humour, and good organisation—talents which she possesses in abundance. She also has no hesitation in using that talent to override procrastinators, doubters, or anything that deters her from the essence of what this charity work is all about; to help those in need through the help of those who aren't.

And her efforts over two decades have not gone unnoticed. In April 1995, Carolyn was awarded the MBE (Member of the British Empire) by Her Majesty Queen Elizabeth II for her services to Thai charities. "But I couldn't collect it at Buckingham Palace until December—because I had the Ploenchit Fair to run."

Which is Carolyn Tarrant in a nutshell; never let an award get in the way of the work you were awarded it for.

With just a week until this year's (1997) Ploenchit Fair, and with a million potential gremlins milling in the system, Carolyn is looking understandably tired. "My husband says I look like an aspirin."

She looks as though she could use one, too. But she simply extracts her coffee mug from the pandemonium she calls her desk and takes a sip. The fax machine beeps. More incoming.

168

But is it all worth it when the day of the fair comes around?

"Absolutely!" she shoots back, energy quickly restored. "I usually leave home at 5 a.m. and tend to wake up the British ambassador at about ten past five. And if not him, then certainly his butler, because he opens the side door for me at the Embassy. Then I put the kettle on." Just like that.

The gates at the Embassy swing open at 5.30 a.m. when the trucks arrive with the tents, toilets, tables, and what have you. "I love it when the stall-holders arrive to set up. Everyone is in such a super mood, and there's great machinations going on as people start unloading and displaying their goods. One year a stall-holder hung her clothes up to change into later, only to discover they'd been given away as a prize."

And every year has it's own menu of dramas. "We've had pick-pockets, lost children, and one year a man had a heart attack after winning the coconut throwing event." I suggest that all that's missing now is a childbirth. She raises her eyes to heaven and from somewhere a dog growls.

"The day *is* fun. To me, it's the end of a lot of hard work, and I enjoy every minute of it. It's very rewarding and I feel a great sense of achievement knowing that I've taken every bean people have and they have enjoyed me doing it. The mood is always upbeat. Like the Hong Kong Sevens, Ploenchit is an event where you bump into people you haven't seen for a year."

And over the years the crowds have grown. "Last year we had 22,000 plus, which was our best year ever. So, one of my problems is actually getting *around* the fair. I have one of these two-way walkie-talkie things which is constantly saying, 'Mrs. Tarrant to stall 91 . . . Mrs. Tarrant you're needed at the wheel of fortune . . .'"

The fact is, Carolyn Tarrant *is* needed because she has so much that people need—energy, perseverance, grit, and wit.

For her, the day flies past as she attends to the duties and pleasures of the fair with a relaxed expertise and an eye on the kids—whose company she enjoys the most. "The day is enriched by a little disorder," she says with a smile.

However, the official part is not over until, "I'm clutching that little bit of paper which tells me the bank take. That's generally about 7 p.m. Then I go and have a drink with the stall-holders and the volunteers who, year after year, are just remarkable."

What is more remarkable is that Carolyn never had to do any of this. She could have lived a comfortable life as the expat wife of a successful husband—doing the social rounds, the official duties, and running a home and staff. Instead, she carved out a purpose built on the rare foundation of selflessness. And there are many who are truly grateful that she has.

She could, and in some ways would like to, pass on the reins of organising this large event to someone else. She feels it's time. But I discover she feels like this every year at this particular juncture—with her phones ringing hot and smoke rising from the fax machine.

Does she really need a motivation to continue?

"No. Because one of my greatest pleasures in life is seeing other people enjoying *their* greatest pleasures in life, and I have always felt very strongly about what we do and what more we can do."

Any expectations for next Saturday?

"I have been told by so many people to expect a thirty per cent drop this year. It *is* a tough time and people are suffering. Our spending power has been reduced dramatically. We ordered a Braille printer that can print hundreds of text books for blind children and schools, but it's doubled in price in the last two months. The donations coming in are less, yet the needs of the charities have increased. There are more street kids, broken homes, drug addicts, and the simply abandoned than ever before."

This year marks the 40th Ploenchit Fair. It is Carolyn's 18th—and the price is still a humble 50 baht.

"Attendance is obligatory," she says with that smile. "Bring lots of money—and spend it."

The Xmas Files 1997

News that never made the news the way other news did.

January: A senior civil servant in the Haryana state of India was charged with having his cook set on fire when he returned late from his holiday.

It was revealed that between 1980 and July 1993, the word "shit" appeared in the *New York Times* just once—in a book review by Paul Theroux.

A scholar discovered that a comic poet from ancient Greece named Cratinus, noticing a rise in corruption, was moved to invent three mock goddesses of bribery—Doro (St. Give), Dexo (St. Receive) and Emblo (St. Backhander).

February: More than 20 million people in Great Britain made telephone calls in an attempt to buy 200 tickets flying on the supersonic Concorde to America for just £10.

In Russia, Prime Minister Mr. Victor Chernomydin, attracted some criticism by shooting two bear cubs and their mother as they came out of hibernation.

Meanwhile, a war with bows and arrows between the Amungme and Dhani tribes in Irian Jaya left five dead.

By the end of the month, an Israeli and an Egyptian had been accused in Cairo of spying for Israel—they had been communicating in messages written in invisible ink on ladies' underwear.

In Spain, the villagers of Manganeses de la Polvorosa, Zamora, threw a goat from their fifty-foot church tower as part of a fiesta tradition—but they caught it unharmed in a tarpaulin.

Snow fell in Lamaca, Cyprus, for the first time since 1950.

March: Electrified barriers, meant to stop rabid foxes coming through the Channel Tunnel, were found to have been out of order for weeks.

In Iran, President Saddam Hussein sued a French journalist for libel for calling him a "perfect cretin."

In Belorussia, border guards found a packet of 300 radioactive American 100-dollar bills being carried by a businessman from Moscow.

Figures revealed that the BBC World Service audience had risen to 143 million.

April: The 194 inmates on death row at Isanya prison in Tanzania, some of whom have been awaiting execution for 15 years, asked to be hanged immediately or set free.

Here in Thailand, Mr. Chavalit Yongchaiyudh, the prime minister, said that articles in the *Bangkok Post* saying that his education minister, Mr. Sukavich Rangsitphol, gave him his daughter as a gift, were getting out of hand.

Names from the Albanian national football squad this month included:

The interpreter, Ilir Agolli.

The manager, Shyqri Rrelli.

The goalkeeper, Blendi Nallbani.

May: A strong earthquake struck off the coast of Mexico. "It generated no wave activity, it didn't hurt anything, and no one felt it," a seismologist said.

In India, the new coalition government promised to reform more than 1,500 Victorian laws, including one which forbids people to go strolling about in frayed clothing.

In the southern hemisphere, a cull began of 1,200 wild horses said to be destroying rare plants on army land in the Kaimanawa Ranges in Central North Island, New Zealand; they were to be turned into dog food.

In Siberia, 406,658 acres of forest were destroyed by fire in 23 days.

June: The Pope, on a visit to Cracow, canonised Queen Hedwig, who died in 1401, aged 25, after marrying a Lithuanian prince at the age of ten.

Over in the US, in Seattle, a man fell 200 feet to his death when his motorised lawn-mower plunged over a cliff at Port Angeles.

July: Exactly 81 years ago this weekend, in 1916, 3,150 men from the South African Brigade entered Delville Wood on the edge of the Somme battlefield in France. After six days of bitter fighting, with artillery fire sometimes arriving at six shells a *second*, they withdrew. 143 men walked out and 1,600 acres of forest ceased to exist; except for one tree, a hornbeam, which still grows there today.

This was also the month when some misconceptions were corrected: Passchendale is not the name of a Californian ice cream, Ulan Bator is not the name of the new Manchester United striker, and Moet Chandon is *not* a shampoo for racing drivers.

August: Eight people were killed by tigers in 19 days in the Lampung province of Indonesia, while in China, explorers discovered a colony of 30 giant pandas in the wilds of Gansu province.

In Japan, 5,168 people reached the 12,400 foot summit of Mt. Fuji on one day, while on the following afternoon, customs men in Russia refused a bribe of US$1 million from smugglers trying to bring in a truck convoy full of vodka from Georgia. (The *idiots*).

Odd weather was everywhere. Hailstones the size of golf balls fell on Gloucestershire in England, while hailstones the size of pigeon's eggs fell on villages east of Madrid.

Narcotics were not to be left out. Police at the Western Mexican port of Colima found more than a ton of cocaine aboard a ship from Columbia. Not long after, the Canadian ambassador resigned after having called Mexico's war on drugs, "A joke."

Ninety-something English thespian, Sir John Gielgud, announced on his birthday, "Most of my friends seem to be either dead, extremely deaf, or living on the wrong side of Kent."

September: At least 4,367 people had been put to death in China.

A small tornado near Newark in Nottinghamshire, England, picked up 40 pigs and threw them half a mile; and in Canada, a 25-stone man from Windsor spent a week stuck in his bath, surviving on tap water before being rescued.

October: The French government introduced legislation to outlaw *"bizutage"* initiation ceremonies—in which students have been forced to eat tadpoles and kiss rotting pig's heads.

A woman in the Mubende district of Uganda brought divorce proceedings against her husband for fear of being eaten—after claiming to have caught him roasting a human leg; whether he actually ate it is not known at this time.

November: It has been estimated that the number of seconds between searches for "sex" on the Internet, is two.

A man calling himself Captain Solo tried to stage a coup in Zambia—but was soon captured.

Beijing blamed a surge in its rat population on the decline in the number of owls, while in Gerona, in Northeast Spain, a computer-dating service for domestic animals opened.

In France, a three-page love letter written by Napoleon Bonaparte to his new wife Josephine, was sold at an auction in Paris for over £65,000.

Still in France, 37 years ago, President Charles de Gaulle declared, "How can you govern a country which has 246 varieties of cheese?" Beats me.

December: The new 24-hour BBC television news service, launched in England with much pizazz, has not been a great success. One in-house producer said, "As far I can tell, it's being watched by 36 people and some battery chickens in a village called Widmerpool."

Exactly a year ago today, an island appeared out of the sea near Tonga, in the Pacific Ocean.

And it's getting bigger.

Happy New Year.

Wealth Behaving Badly

"We've had nothing to do with our own evolution,
but have had everything to do with our own decline."
Gabriel Garcia Marquez.

We met by chance outside the new British Library in London, which, incidentally, is a hideous building. Everything about it screams, "Go Away." It's as if the SS Waffen had gone into real estate.

Later, in a London nightclub where the people and the music were both impenetrable and overwhelming, my friend told me his tale. The last time I had heard from him was in 1972, when he sent me a Christmas card from Africa which read, *"Bingo, Bango, Bongo, I'm just so happy in the Congo."*

But not that happy, apparently. He had soon returned to the UK and went into the City—that square mile of Central London where money is moved, made, and lost in amounts that resemble galactic phone numbers. At his peak, at just 26 years old, he was on £100,000 a year with a bonus of up to and beyond a cool £1 million.

"I knew I'd made it," he said, "when I woke one dawn and found myself at the wheel of my Aston Martin, which had somehow found *itself* in a ditch just outside Oxford. I vaguely remembered a terrific party the night before. There and then, I decided I was going to wear a dinner jacket for the rest of my life."

In the end he blew the lot—on wild boar shoots and a 36DD lingerie model. "And I don't regret it for an instant," he added, with conviction.

He had put on a lot of bulk. "Like Count Dracula," he confessed, "I have developed the irritating habit of eating between meals." He was also chemically challenged, morally relaxed, and way beyond a little help from his friends. He had also reached a stage where he suffered from serious delays in retrieving stored information—and when he *did* manage to retrieve it, it was always ten minutes too late. But again, no regrets. If nothing else, his ironies had at least remained intact.

As the club's band, Bushmen Don't Surf, blundered into their second set, he dashed out and soon returned with nine Mars Bars and a Christmas present for me wrapped in the *London Evening Standard*.

"It's from Bulgaria," he said excitedly.

He'd bought me a Russian Princess Diana doll. Beneath Diana were revealed ever smaller dolls of Dodi, Henri Paul, the two princes, and then, finally, a little mangled Mercedes. Sick, yes—but sales were stratospheric.

It should be noted that some City traders have appalling taste, yet like pioneering rock stars, they manage to pack more into a single decade than most ordinary mortals do in an entire lifetime.

What I do resent, however, is being cornered by a trader or a member of the *nouveau* poor in a Bangkok bar, who lived a life of almost surreal luxury during the good times, and now says that his suffering is worse than mine. Well, it isn't, and you know it isn't by the very tone in which he assures you it is.

When the sensuous cocktail of cheap loans and deep credit finally met at the crest of bull and confidence, it was like one of those fortuitous blind dates when the right place meets the right time. In Bangkok, there was a secondary futures market in restaurant tables alone. The volume was deafening, the elbows invasive, and the privilege dripped like the well-adjusted jewellery that the new wealth had paid for.

Someone should have spotted it.

The press did their best, the politicians their worst, and cheques continued to be written. The authorities would turn a blind eye, and suddenly no one could remember a fucking thing.

The *nouveau riche* wanted to be taken seriously because they had, well, *pretensions*. It was a time to act your credit limit, not your real age. And then, on that fateful July 2nd, the "hi-so" were suddenly the so-so, and the so-so will soon be the so-what. Easy come easy go. Anything that makes you feel that good is bound to drag you down. Now they have been reduced to extras in their own story, and their only language is tears, loss of face, and "due dates."

What's more interesting is that those now deprived of their unearned wealth have become dysfunctional, and seem to exist on amoebic auxiliary power. They might not have heard the gong, but they sure as hell felt the echo.

Yet the pursuit of wealth and power has always seemed to me to be a religion that starts off relieving your pain, and ends up causing it. Just look at the cunning primate who runs Iraq—Sadman Insane. A perfect example.

The danger of worshipping money for its own sake is that, take it away, and the whole fabric falls apart. There is no substance behind it. The trend of the *nouveau riche* in Thailand was to spend money they didn't really have, on things they really didn't need, to impress people they didn't even like. Result? They paid with their souls. The fact that Buddhism believes in the "self" rather than the soul was extremely fortunate. Whatever. The sharp and connected never felt a thing anyway, having got their money out days before the crash, thereby doubling their wealth. Timing is everything.

And yet no one will take any responsibility. Which is like saying, "I didn't lose my virginity. I just misplaced it."

The rich almost got away with it. But like Bill Clinton, they made a fatal mistake—there was always a gap between principle and reality. And like the US President, politically they were nearly convincing, morally nearly repulsive, and legally nearly guilty. Hey, they even *nearly* smoked marijuana. In each case, both he and they never quite committed, keeping one small part of themselves from any clear or definitive loyalty. So they could blame everyone but themselves in retrospect. Very British that, by the way.

It was all volume and no bass. All appetite and no hunger. On a dramatic level it may have been exciting, but on a human level, it's a long walk back to the changing rooms.

Yet money knows all about God, because it behaves in exactly the same way as God. It's omnipotent, omnipresent, and timeless. It can work miracles and wake the dead. It can cure the sick, and make happy endings. It can judge and punish. And it answers prayers all day, everyday. But it knows it's all a con trick; a sleight of hand that's computer-enhanced. And at the same time, it believes it—which is precisely the problem.

So. Let's pause and consider. Should we therefore applaud clever entrepreneurs for a job well done, for generating invisible earnings for Thailand, for picking up a fair wage for long hours at the dealing screens? Or are they parasites on the national interest, encouraging damaging short-termism, while being arrogant, over-paid, and over-indulgent? The choice is surely yours, but the decision defines your values.

There was an 18th century European fad of going to laugh at lunatics in asylums for entertainment. Perhaps it's time to revive it, and to put the people who have plundered this country into cages and go do the same.

Take the kids. It would be both fun and educational.

Caught in the Fact

I know we might all be going to hell in a balloon, but don't you just love how the spin doctors have come up with a "managed float" to describe the trip? Either the ticket seller has a light touch or it's being flown by a pilot of delusion. And what's this "defacto devaluation?" Is that two live-in lovers downgraded to a blind date?

Let's be clear about this. It isn't the figures that got us into this mess, it was the words spoken by the people who allowed it to happen.

"Listen up. We'll borrow some kroners that will upset the peso and mortify the lira, and bring in sacks of shekels to build a dollar-funded hotel just like our friends did. Baht for baht, we'll be better off."

"Sure Somchai, whatever you say."

"Especially if we put it in your wife's name."

"No problem."

"What *is* her name?"

"Franca."

"Of course it is. We'll use some of those too."

Words matter. To develop an interest in your own language is advisable and, ultimately, crucial. For if you cannot say what you mean, you will never mean what you say.

Consequently, the word "recession" shouldn't bother freelance writers as the majority of them have spent their entire lives in one. Security has never even been the issue, survival has. Some writers are masters at it. I have a colleague in London who writes about the economy. He's never out of a job because he makes finance mysterious by showing how mysterious finance is. His page is a blizzard of statistics and his eyes are often the colour of Guinness.

But they should not try to be too clever, as Mr. Wilde once pointed out: "*Andiaorocte* is the title of a volume of poems by the Reverend Clarence Walworth. It is a word borrowed from the Indian and should, we think, be returned to them as soon as possible."

Even in the best of times, when currencies are humming a carefree tune, it's never been easy for a writer to break into the market. In the past, rejection was at least accompanied by manners: "Sir, your manuscript is both good and original. Unfortunately, where it is good it is not original, and where it is original it is not good."

And there are venerable hacks out there who still believe that writers should be made to ferret around for their livelihood, inserting themselves by their own efforts into the interstices of the market, turning their words into *satang*, while hanging onto solvency by their fingernails. Their work is all the better for being produced in anxiety, and even want, by a combination of desperado, low cunning, and impudent braggadocio. Without hunger, many have written little.

Don't you just hate people who are right?

Still, writers, like all artists, usually spend at least some part of their lives congregating cheek by jowl in unwholesome rookeries chosen for cheapness and convenience. I still do. Such literary menageries have existed in London and Paris since the 16th century. Penny-a-liners lived in bare-boarded garrets not far from the printers den in which they wheedled a living from the hardfaced publishers. Gin was a penny a pint.

If that wasn't enough to put a young scribe off for good, writers once had to make their own pens, which, in essence, were goose quills crafted into a nib which scritched across the coarse paper so loudly you could hear it in the next area code. (Hey! It's 2 a.m.! Turn that damn writing *down*!). Brushes for their illustrations were made with hairs from their own head, and from the hides of pigs and cattle. Many lived in crazy isolation. Well maybe, but I couldn't possibly comment about that.

And isn't it just typical? Success does not always guarantee happiness or even fulfillment. As one writer remarked: "Being published by the Oxford University Press is rather like being married to a duchess; the honour is almost greater than the pleasure."

Likewise, frustration at trying to complete something is equally a hassle, as the English author P. G. Wodehouse noted in the cover of one of his manuscripts: "To my daughter Leanora, without whose never failing sympathy and encouragement this book would have been written in half the time."

Writers are often accused of being overtly sensitive and just too precious about their work—and rightly so. But perhaps they are not quite as egotistical as rock stars. Michael Jackson? He doesn't need an audience, he needs a mirror.

But as a breed, writers generally hate being edited, even though they may grumpily admit to needing it. As with most writers who have been subjected to the process, Thomas Jefferson thought the final text of his Declaration of Independence depressingly inferior to his original. And, like most writers, he was wrong. Indeed, seldom had a writer been better served. Congress had the wisdom to leave untouched those sections that were unimprovable—notably the opening—and threw out much that was irrelevant. The new constitution of Thailand certainly needs a good editor, but I think many will happily settle for divine intervention.

And by the way, writers do not get writers block, they just fall into a linguistic coma.

Sometimes a translation can provide a new angle, if not a whole new meaning to an event. A friend who works at the *Thai Rath* newspaper, told me that on the day the TWA airliner crashed into the ocean shortly after take off from New York, the paper printed an unprecedented three lines for the header:

GIANT PLANE CRASH.
BOMB WENT BANG.
EVERYBODY DEAD.

Ouch! Yet, I like the company of writers and those people who work in newspapers. They are amusing and gossipy and clever. And it is nourishing to be among men and women of literary voltage—the type that can wrap up life in a sentence and still keep a deadline.

For it should always be remembered that there are no bad words, only inexperienced users.

*The most fetching
and recent thing
we could find.*